"十四五"高等院校经济管理类课程实验指导丛书

公司金融
实验课教程

CORPORATE

FINANCE

EXPERIMENT

COURSE

李 薇◎编著

经济管理出版社
ECONOMY & MANAGEMENT PUBLISHING HOUSE

图书在版编目（CIP）数据

公司金融实验课教程／李薇编著. —北京：经济管理出版社，2021.7
ISBN 978-7-5096-8162-6

I. ①公… II. ①李… III. ①公司—金融学—实验—高等学校—教材 IV. ①F276.6-33

中国版本图书馆 CIP 数据核字（2021）第 145192 号

组稿编辑：王光艳
责任编辑：高　娅　王东霞
责任印制：黄章平
责任校对：陈晓霞

出版发行：经济管理出版社
　　　　　（北京市海淀区北蜂窝 8 号中雅大厦 A 座 11 层　100038）
网　　　址：www. E-mp. com. cn
电　　　话：（10）51915602
印　　　刷：北京晨旭印刷厂
经　　　销：新华书店
开　　　本：720mm×1000mm /16
印　　　张：14
字　　　数：251 千字
版　　　次：2021 年 7 月第 1 版　　2021 年 7 月第 1 次印刷
书　　　号：ISBN 978-7-5096-8162-6
定　　　价：68.00 元

前言

Preface

　　公司金融，作为高等院校金融学专业开设的一门重要专业课，既有很强的理论性也有极严格的实践要求。随着我国金融业的开放和经济金融领域国际交往与合作的日益密切，市场对具有较高英语水平的专业人才需求增加。在此背景下，本教程系统地把公司金融理论与实验有机结合，形成了内容充实、系统完整、简明实用的双语实验教学体系，希望在公司金融理论的基础上全面培养学生的实验技能和实践能力。

　　教材内容按照资金在公司内部的流动顺序，依次介绍公司融资的渠道与决策、公司投资决策和财务数据分析等方面的内容，并对时间价值、年金、分期付款、资本结构、收益与风险、资产组合等知识点设置实验。本书面向金融学或财务管理专业本科生，是一本双语教学的简明实验课教材。

　　鉴于时间和编者学识有限，不足之处敬请同行专家和诸位读者批评指正。

李　薇

2020 年 8 月

目录

Contents

Part One   Financial   Fundations
(金融基础)

Part Two　Financing
（融资）

Part Three　Investment
（投资）

Part Four   Financial Analysis (财务分析)

Part One

Financial Fundations
(金融基础)

Chapter 1
The Time Value of Money
(资金的时间价值)

1.1　Compound Interest（复利计息）

In business, there is probably no other concept with more power or applications than that of the time value of money (TVM). So, it is essential for you to have a clear understanding of the time value of money.

1.1.1　Time Value of Money Concept（资金的时间价值概念）

It's a fundamental concept in finance that money has a time value associated with it：A dollar received today is worth more than a dollar received a year from now.

Intuitively this idea is easy to understand. We are all familiar with the concept of interest. Because we can earn interest on money received today, it is better to receive money earlier rather than later.

In other words, in order to assign time value to money, it must be possible to invest money at a positive rate of return.

1.1.2　Time Lines（时间线）

One of the most important tools in time value analysis is the time line. A time line is simply a diagram of the cash flows associated with a TVM problem, which is used by analysts to visualize what is happening in a particular problem and set up the problem for solution.

So it is often a good idea to draw a time line before you start to solve a TVM problem (see Figure 1-1).

Figure 1-1 A Time Line for Five Periods

Time 0 is today (present). Time 1 is one period from today. Time 2 is two periods from today, or the end of period 2. Often the periods are years, but other time intervals such as semiannual periods, quarters, months, or even days can aslo be used.

Note that each point mark corresponds to the end of one period as well as the beginning of the next period. For example, the point mark at Time 1 represents the end of period 1, and it also represents the beginning of period 2 because period 1 has just passed.

Then we will add each cash flow to the very point on time line according to when it happens. A cash flow that occurs in the present (today) is put to Time 0. Cash outflows (payments) are given a negative sign, and cash inflows (receipts) are given a positive sign.

Example: Please illustrate a time line for an investment that costs $100 today and will return a stream of cash payments of $30 per year at the end of each of the next 5 years.

Answer: As shown by Figure 1-2.

Figure 1-2 A Time Line with Cash Payments of $30 for Five Years

Example: Please illustrate a time line for an investment that costs $100 today and will return a stream of cash payments of $25 at the end of year 1, $35 at the beginning of year 3, $45 at the end of year 3, $15 at the beginning of year 5, $55 at the end of year 5.

Answer: As shown by Figure 1-3.

Figure 1-3   A Time Line with Increasing Payments for Five Years

When we face up to a real TVM problem, the interest rate should be added. Cash flows are placed directly below the point marks, and interest rates are shown directly above the time line. Unknown cash flows, which you are trying to find in the analysis, are indicated by question marks.

Now consider this situation, where a $100 cash outflow is made today, and the interest rate is 5 percent during the first three periods, then it rises to 10 percent during the forth and fifth period, so how much will we receive at the end of Time 5?

You can visualize the problem by the time line shown as follows (see Figure 1-4):

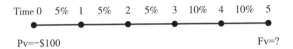

Figure 1-4   A Time Line with Different Interest Rates for Five Years

1.1.3   Compound Interest (复利)[①]

The notion of compound interest or interest on interest is deeply embedded in TVM procedures. Compound interest occurs when interest (利息) paid is added to the principal (本金). When an investment is subjected to compound interest, the growth in the value of the investment from period to period reflects not only the interest earned on the original principal amount but also the interest earned on the previous period's interest earnings, that is interest on interest.

For example, we place $100 in a savings account that pays 8 percent interest compounded annually. How will our savings grow?

---

① 资金的时间价值一般都是按复利进行计算的。所谓复利，是指不仅本金要计算利息，利息也要计算利息，即通常所说的"利滚利"。

At the end of first year we will earn 8 percent interest, that is:

$$FV_1 = PV(1+i)$$
$$= \$100(1+8\%) \tag{1-1}$$
$$= \$108$$

Carrying these calculations one period further, we find that we now earn the 8 percent interest on a principal of $100 (including the original principal $100 and the first-year interest $8), that is:

$$FV_2 = FV_1(1+i) \tag{1-2}$$

Which, for our example, is:

$$FV_2 = \$108(1+8\%)$$
$$= \$116.64$$

If we substitute equation (1-1) into equation (1-2), we get:

$$FV_2 = PV(1+i)(1+i)$$
$$= PV(1+i)^2 \tag{1-3}$$

We can generalize a formula to illustrate the value of our investment if it is compounded annually at a rate of i for n years:

$$FV_n = PV(1+i)^n \tag{1-4}$$

Where:

FV_n = the future value of the investment at the end of n years

n = the number of years during which the compounding occurs

i = the annual interest rate

PV = the present value or original amount invested at the beginning of the first year

Table 1-1 illustrates how this investment of $100 would continue to grow for the first 10 years at a compound interest rate of 8 percent.

Table 1-1 Illustration of Compound Interest with $100 Initial Investment and 8 Percent Annual Interest

Period	Beginning Value ($)	Interest Earned During Period ($)	Terminal Value ($)
1	100.00	8.00	108.00

Continued

Period	Beginning Value ($)	Interest Earned During Period ($)	Terminal Value ($)
2	108.00	8.64	116.64
3	116.64	9.33	125.97
4	125.97	10.08	136.05
5	136.05	10.88	146.93
6	146.93	11.76	158.69
7	158.69	12.69	171.38
8	171.38	13.71	185.09
9	185.09	14.81	199.90
10	199.90	15.99	215.89

1.1.4 Fractional Periods (不完整期间)

In our illustrations, we have computed the future value for whole years. Then, what about an investment is made for part of a year?

For example, suppose that $100 is invested for 7 years and three months. What is the future value at the end of the period?

Since 3 months is 0.25 of 1 year, n in the future value formula (1-4) is 7.25. Assuming an annual interest rate of 5%, the future value of $100 invested for 7 years and 3 months is $142.437, as shown below:

$$PV = \$100$$
$$i = 0.05$$
$$n = 7.25$$

$$FV = \$100 \ (1.05)^{7.25}$$
$$= \$100 \ (1.424369)$$
$$= \$142.437$$

1.1.5 Compounding More than One Time Per Year (一年多次计息)[①]

Up to now, we have assumed that interest is paid annually. While, what if we compound the interest more than once per year.

In fact, interest may be paid semiannually, quarterly, monthly, weekly, or daily. To begin with, let's suppose interest is paid semiannually (半年计息) and \$100 is deposited in an account at 8 percent. This means that for the first 6 months the return is one half of 8 percent, or 4 percent. Thus, the future value (FV) at the end of 6 months will be:

$$FV_{1/2} = \$100(1+\frac{0.08}{2}) = \$104.00$$

And at the end of a year it will be:

$$FV_1 = FV_{1/2}(1+\frac{0.08}{2})$$

$$FV_1 = \$100(1+\frac{0.08}{2})^2 = \$108.16$$

Comparing this amonnt with \$108.00 when interest is paid only once a year, there is a \$0.16 difference attribu table to the fact that during the second 6 months, interest is earned on the \$4.00 interest paid at the end of the first 6 months.

To continue, let's suppose interest is paid quarterly (季度计息) and we will again find out the future value at the end of 1 year. It would be:

$$FV_1 = \$100(1+\frac{0.08}{4})(1+\frac{0.08}{4})(1+\frac{0.08}{4})(1+\frac{0.08}{4})$$

$$FV_1 = \$100(1+\frac{0.08}{4})^4 = \$108.24$$

Which, of course, is higher than it would have been with semiannual or annual compounding.

---

① 一年多次计息。在前面的讨论中，利息是一年计一次的，但实际上，利息可以半年计一次、每季度计一次（一年四次）、每月计一次（一年十二次）或者一年计多次，计息次数的不同会影响资金的实际收益率，我们将在后面的内容里作具体的解释。

The future value at the end of 3 years for the example with quarterly interest payments is:

$$FV_3 = \$ 100 \ (1 + \frac{0.08}{4})^{4 \times 3} = \$ 126.82$$

While a terminal value with semiannual compounding is:

$$FV_3 = \$ 100 \ (1 + \frac{0.08}{2})^{2 \times 3} = \$ 126.53$$

And with annual compounding is:

$$FV_3 = \$ 100 \ (1 + \frac{0.08}{1})^{1 \times 3} = \$ 125.97$$

To Sum up, the greater the number of years, the greater the difference in terminal values between two different methods of compounding.

Mathematically, we can express the future value when interest is paid m times per year as follows:

$$FV_n = PV \ (1 + \frac{i}{m})^{mn} \tag{1-5}$$

Where:

i = annual interest rate

n = number of years

m = times per year the interest is paid

From the formula we can see, the more times during a year that interest is paid, the greater the terminal value at the end of a given year.

Example: Suppose that a portfolio manager makes an investment of \$ 1 million that promises to pay an annual interest rate of 10% for 6 years. Interest on this investment is paid quarterly. What is the future value?

Answer:

PV = \$ 1000000

n = 6

i = 0.10

m = 4

$$FV_n = PV \left(1 + \frac{i}{m}\right)^{mn}$$

$$FV_6 = \$\,1000000 \left(1 + \frac{0.10}{4}\right)^{4 \times 6}$$

$$= \$\,1808726$$

1.1.6 Continuous Compounding (连续复利)

In the formula $FV_n = PV \left(1 + \frac{i}{m}\right)^{mn}$, as m approaches infinity, the term $\left(1 + \frac{i}{m}\right)^{mn}$ approaches $e^{i \times n}$[①], where e is approximately 2.71828.

So, the terminal value at the end of n years of an initial deposit of PV where interest is compounded continuously at a rate of i is:

$$FV = PV \times e^{i \times n} \tag{1-6}$$

1.1.7 Effective Annual Rate (实际年利率)

Financial institutions usually quote rates as stated annual interest rates (名义年利率), or nominal rates, along with a compounding frequency, as opposed to quoting rates as periodic rates (the rate of interest earned over a single compounding period).

For example, a bank will quote a savings rate as 8 percent compounded quarterly, rather than 2 percent per quarter. The rate of interest that investors actually realize as a result of compounding is known as the effective annual rate (EAR).

EAR represents the annual rate of return actually being earned after adjustments have been made for different compounding periods.

EAR may be determined as follows:

$$EAR = \left(1 + \frac{i}{m}\right)^{m} - 1 \text{[②]} \tag{1-7}$$

----

① As $e = \lim\limits_{m \to \infty} \left(1 + \frac{1}{m}\right)^{m}$, so $\lim\limits_{m \to \infty} \left(1 + \frac{i}{m}\right)^{m \times n} = \lim\limits_{m \to \infty} \left[\left(1 + \frac{i}{m}\right)^{\frac{m}{i} \times i \times n}\right] = \lim\limits_{m \to \infty} \left[\left(1 + \frac{i}{m}\right)^{\frac{m}{i}}\right]^{i \times n} = e^{i \times n}$.

② To invest $\$\,1$ at i for one year compounding m times, will actually get $\$\,1 \left(1 + \frac{i}{m}\right)^{m \times 1}$, so its actual rate of return is $\dfrac{\$\,1\left(1 + \frac{i}{m}\right)^{m \times 1} - \$\,1}{\$\,1}$, that is EAR $= \left(1 + \frac{i}{m}\right)^{m} - 1$.

Where:

$$i = \text{annual interest rate}$$

$$m = \text{times per year the interest is paid}$$

Obviously, whenever compound interest is being used, the stated rate and the effective (actual) rate of interest are equal only when interest is compounded annually ($m=1$). Otherwise, the EAR is greater than the stated rate.

Example: Using a stated rate of 6 percent, compute EARs for semiannual, quarterly, monthly, daily, and continuous compounding.

Answer:

$$\text{Semiannual effective rate} = (1+\frac{0.06}{2})^2 - 1 = 1.06090 - 1$$

$$= 0.06090 = 6.090\%$$

$$\text{Quarterly effective rate} = (1+\frac{0.06}{4})^4 - 1 = 1.06136 - 1$$

$$= 0.06136 = 6.136\%$$

$$\text{Monthly effective rate} = (1+\frac{0.06}{12})^{12} - 1 = 1.06168 - 1$$

$$= 0.06168 = 6.168\%$$

$$\text{Daily effective rate} = (1+\frac{0.06}{365})^{365} - 1 = 1.06183 - 1$$

$$= 0.06183 = 6.183\%$$

$$\text{Continuous effective rate} = e^{0.06} - 1 = 1.06184 - 1$$

$$= 0.06184 = 6.184\%$$

1.2　Future Value and Present Value (终值和现值)

1.2.1　Future Value (终值)

Future value is the amount to which a current deposit will grow over time when it is placed in an account paying compound interest.

The process to computing FVs involves projecting the cash flows forward, on the basis of an appropriate compound interest rate, to the end of the investment's life.

The process of going from today's values, or present values (*PVs*) to future values (*FVs*) is called compounding.

The formula for finding the FV of a single cash flow is:

$$FV_n = PV \left(1 + \frac{i}{m}\right)^{mn} \tag{1-8}$$

Where:

PV = the present value or original amount invested

at the beginning of the first year

n = the number of years during which the compounding occurs

i = the annual interest rate

m = times per year the interest is paid

As the determination of future value can be quite time-consuming when an investment is held for a number of years, the **future value interest factor** ($FVIF_{i,n}$)[①] defined as $(1+i)^n$, has been compiled for various value of i and n. The future value interest factor are shown in Table 1-2. Note that the compounding factors given in this table represent the value of \$1 compounded at rate i at the end of the n_{th} year. Thus, to calculate the future value of an initial investment, we only need to determine the $FVIF_{i,n}$, then multiply it by the initial investment. In effect, we can rewrite equation (1-8) as follows:

$$FV_n = PV(FVIF_{i,n}) \tag{1-9}$$

Table 1-2　Future Value Interest Factor ($FVIF_{i,n}$) for \$1 Compounded at Rate i for n Periods

n (Period)	1%	2%	3%	4%	5%	6%	7%	8%	9%	10%
1	1.010	1.020	1.030	1.040	1.050	1.060	1.070	1.080	1.090	1.100
2	1.020	1.040	1.061	1.082	1.103	1.124	1.145	1.166	1.188	1.210
3	1.030	1.061	1.093	1.125	1.158	1.191	1.225	1.260	1.295	1.331

---

① 复利终值系数。

Continued

n (Period)	1%	2%	3%	4%	5%	6%	7%	8%	9%	10%
4	1.041	1.082	1.126	1.170	1.216	1.262	1.311	1.360	1.412	1.464
5	1.051	1.104	1.159	1.217	1.276	1.338	1.403	1.469	1.539	1.611
6	1.062	1.126	1.194	1.265	1.340	1.419	1.501	1.587	1.677	1.772
7	1.072	1.149	1.230	1.316	1.407	1.504	1.606	1.714	1.828	1.949
8	1.083	1.172	1.267	1.369	1.477	1.594	1.718	1.851	1.993	2.144
9	1.094	1.195	1.305	1.423	1.551	1.689	1.838	1.999	2.172	2.358
10	1.105	1.219	1.344	1.480	1.629	1.791	1.967	2.159	2.367	2.594
11	1.116	1.243	1.384	1.539	1.710	1.898	2.105	2.332	2.580	2.853
12	1.127	1.268	1.426	1.601	1.796	2.012	2.252	2.518	2.813	3.138
13	1.138	1.294	1.469	1.665	1.886	2.133	2.410	2.720	3.066	3.452
14	1.149	1.319	1.513	1.732	1.980	2.261	2.579	2.937	3.342	3.797
15	1.161	1.346	1.558	1.801	2.079	2.397	2.759	3.172	3.642	4.177

Example: If we invest \$ 500 in a bank where it will earn 8 percent compounded annually, how much will it be worth at the end of seven years?

Answer:

Looking at Table 1-2 in the row $n = 7$ and column $i = 8\%$, we find that $FVIF_{8\%,7}$ has a value of 1.714, so we find:

$$FV_n = PV(FVIF_{8\%,7})$$
$$= \$ 500(1.714)$$
$$= \$ 857$$

Example: If we invest \$ 500 in a bank where it will earn 8 percent compounded quarterly, how much will it be worth at the end of two years?

Answer:

Looking at Table 1-2 in the row $n = 2 \times 4 = 8$ and column $i = 8\%/4 = 2\%$, we find that $FVIF_{2\%,8}$ has a value of 1.172, so:

$$FV_n = PV(FVIF_{2\%,8})$$
$$= \$ 500(1.172)$$
$$= \$ 586$$

1.2.2　Present Value（现值）

Up until this point we have been moving money forward in time line. We are now going to look at the reverse question: what is the value in today's dollars of a sum of money to be received in the future?

The *PV* of a single sum is today's value of a cash flow that is to be received at some point in the future. In other words, it is the amount of money that must be invested today, at a given rate of return over a given period of time, in order to end up with a specified *FV*.

The process for finding the *PV* of a cash flow is known as discounting (future cash flows are "discounted" back to the present). The interest rate used in the discounting process is commonly referred to as discounting rate (贴现率).

Recall from the previous part that the future value of a sum invested for *n* years and compounded *m* times, can be expressed as:

$$FV_n = PV\left(1+\frac{i}{m}\right)^{mn}$$

Rewriting the above equation to solve for PV, we get:

$$PV = \frac{FV_n}{\left(1+\frac{i}{m}\right)^{mn}} \tag{1-10}$$

Example: If you need \$500 two years later, and your bank permits a 8 percent interest rate compounded annually, so how much should you deposit now?

Answer:

$$FV = \$500$$

$$n = 2$$

$$i = 0.08$$

$$m = 1$$

$$PV = \frac{FV_n}{\left(1+\frac{i}{m}\right)^{mn}}$$

$$PV = \frac{\$ 500}{(1+\frac{0.08}{1})^{1\times2}}$$

$$= \$ 429$$

When interest is compounded more than once a year, for example, the present value of $100 to be received at the end of year 3 with the discount rate being 10 percent compounded quarterly is:

$$PV = \frac{\$ 100}{(1+\frac{0.10}{4})^{4\times3}} = \$ 74.36$$

If a future value is to be received or paid over a fractional part of a year, the number of years is adjusted accordingly.

Example: If $1000 is to be received 9 years and 3 months from now and the interest rate is 7%, what's the present value?

Answer:

$$FV = \$ 1000$$

$$i = 7\%$$

$$n = 9.25$$

$$PV = \$ 1000 \left[\frac{1}{(1+0.07)^{9.25}} \right]$$

$$= \$ 534.81$$

Example: Compute the FV and PV of a $1000 single sum and an investment horizon of one year using a stated annual interest rate of 6.0 percent with a range of compounding periods.

Answer: As shown by Table 1-3.

Table 1-3   The Effect of Compounding Frequency on FV and PV

Compounding Frequency	Interest Rate per Period (%)	Effective Rate of Interest (%)	FV ($)	PV ($)
Annual	6.000	6.000	1060.00	943.396
Semiannual	3.000	6.090	1060.90	942.596

Continued

Compounding Frequency	Interest Rate per Period（%）	Effective Rate of Interest（%）	FV（$）	PV（$）
Quarterly	1.500	6.136	1061.36	942.184
Monthly	0.500	6.168	1061.68	941905
Daily	0.016	6.183	1061.83	941.769

To aid in the computation of present values, the present value interest factor（$PVIF_{i,n}$）[1], defined as $\left[\dfrac{1}{(1+\frac{i}{m})^{mn}}\right]$, has been compiled for various combinations of n and i in Table 1-4. A close examination of this equation shows that the values are merely the inverse of those found in Table 1-2.

Table 1-4　Present Value Interest Factor（$PVIF_{i,n}$）for ＄1 Compounded at Rate i for n Periods

n（Period）	1%	2%	3%	4%	5%	6%	7%	8%	9%	10%
1	0.990	0.980	0.971	0.962	0.952	0.943	0.935	0.926	0.917	0.909
2	0.980	0.961	0.943	0.925	0.907	0.890	0.873	0.857	0.842	0.826
3	0.971	0.942	0.915	0.889	0.864	0.840	0.816	0.794	0.772	0.751
4	0.961	0.924	0.888	0.855	0.823	0.792	0.763	0.735	0.708	0.683
5	0.951	0.906	0.863	0.822	0.784	0.747	0.713	0.681	0.650	0.621
6	0.942	0.888	0.837	0.790	0.746	0.705	0.666	0.630	0.596	0.564
7	0.933	0.871	0.813	0.760	0.711	0.655	0.623	0.583	0.547	0.513
8	0.923	0.853	0.789	0.731	0.677	0.627	0.582	0.540	0.502	0.467
9	0.914	0.837	0.766	0.703	0.645	0.592	0.544	0.500	0.460	0.424
10	0.905	0.820	0.744	0.676	0.614	0.558	0.508	0.463	0.422	0.386
11	0.896	0.804	0.722	0.650	0.585	0.527	0.475	0.429	0.388	0.350

① 复利现值系数。

Continued

n (Period)	1%	2%	3%	4%	5%	6%	7%	8%	9%	10%
12	0. 887	0. 788	0. 701	0. 625	0. 557	0. 497	0. 444	0. 397	0. 356	0. 319
13	0. 879	0. 773	0. 681	0. 601	0. 530	0. 469	0. 415	0. 368	0. 326	0. 290
14	0. 870	0. 758	0. 661	0. 577	0. 505	0. 442	0. 388	0. 340	0. 299	0. 263
15	0. 861	0. 743	0. 642	0. 555	0. 481	0. 417	0. 362	0. 315	0. 275	0. 239

Now, to determine the present value of a sum of money to be received at some future date, we only need to determine the value of the appropriate $PVIF_{i,n}$, and multiply it by the future value. In effect we can use our new notation and rewrite equation (1–10) as follows:

$$PV = FV_n(PVIF_{i,n}) \qquad (1\text{–}11)$$

Example: What is the present value of $1500 to be received at the end of 10 years if discount rate is 8 percent compounded annually?

Answer: Looking at Table 1–4 in the row $n = 10$ and column $i = 8\%$, we find that $PVIF_{8\%,10}$ has a value of 0. 463, so we get:

$$PV = \$ 1500(0. 463)$$
$$= \$ 694. 50$$

Example: What is the present value of $1500 to be received at the end of 4 years if discount rate is 8 percent compounded semiannually?

Answer: Looking at Table 1–4 in the row $n = 2 \times 4 = 8$ and column $i = 8\%/2 = 4\%$, we find that $PVIF_{4\%,8}$ has a value of 0. 731, so we get:

$$PV = \$ 1500(0. 731)$$
$$= \$ 1096. 50$$

At this point, you should realize that compounding and discounting are related, and by dealing with one equation $FV_n = PV(1+i)^n$, we can solve for either the FV or the PV.

You see, there are four variables in this equation—FV, PV, i and n, and if you know the values of any three, you can find the value of the fourth.

Example: Solving for i

Suppose you can buy a security at a price of $80. 00, and it will pay you $100 after five years, what is your rate of return? Here you know *FV*, *PV* and *n*, and you want to find *i*—The interest rate you would earn if you bought the security. Such problems are solved as follows.

Answer:

$FV = \$100$

$PV = \$80$

$n = 5$

$$FV_n = PV(1+i)^n$$

$$\$100 = \$80.00(1+i)^5$$

$$i = 4.564\%$$

Example: Solving for *n*

Suppose you invest $80.00 at an interest rate of 4.564 percent per year. How long will it take your investment to grow to $100?

Answer:

$FV = \$100$

$PV = \$80$

$i = 0.04564$

$$FV_n = PV(1+i)^n$$

$$\$100 = \$80.00(1+0.04564)^n$$

$$n = 5$$

Experiment 1
Excel Implementation for
Time Value Problem

一、使用 NPV 函数解决资金现值问题

例 1：如果利率或贴现率为 8%，三年末的 1000 元的现值是多少？

例 2：如果利率或贴现率为 8%，第 1 年末、第 2 年末、第 3 年末的现金流分别为 1000 元、800 元、400 元，则这三笔资金的现值和是多少？

以上问题可用如下模型解决（见表 1-5）。

表 1-5　用 NPV 函数求解资金现值

	B	C	D	E	F
1	单笔资金现值问题				
2	利率	8.00%			
3	期数	金额			
4	1	0.00			
5	2	0.00			
6	3	1000.00			
7	现值	793.83	=NPV(C2,C4:C6)		
8					
9					
10	数笔不等资金现值问题				
11	利率	8.00%			
12	期数	金额			
13	1	1000.00			
14	2	800.00			
15	3	400.00			
16	现值	1929.33	=NPV(C11,C13:C15)		
17					

二、使用 EXCEL 解决终值问题

例3：当前1000元本金，年利率10%，则按复利计算第10年末的终值是多少（见表1-6）？

表1-6　用复利公式或资金流量表求解单笔资金终值

	I	J	K	L	M	N
19	3. 单笔资金终值					
20	利率	10%		=J22*$J$20		
21	期数	期初值	利息	本息和	=J22+K22	
22	0	1000.00	100.00	1100.00		
23	1	1100.00	110.00	1210.00		
24	=L22　　2	1210.00	121.00	1331.00		
25	3	1331.00	133.10	1464.10		
26	4	1464.10	146.41	1610.51		
27	5	1610.51	161.05	1771.56		
28	6	1771.56	177.16	1948.72		
29	7	1948.72	194.87	2143.59		
30	8	2143.59	214.36	2357.95		
31	9	2357.95	235.79	2593.74		
32	10	2593.74				
33		或者:=J22*(1+J20)^10				
34						

Chapter 2
Annuities
(年金)

2.1 Annuities (年金)^①

An annuity is a stream of equal cash flows that occur at equal intervals over a given period. There are two types of annuities: ordinary annuities and annuities due.

The ordinary annuity（普通年金）is the most common type of annuity. It is characterized by cash flows that occur at the end of each compounding period②.

The other type of annuity is called an annuity due（先付年金）, where payments or receipts occur at the beginning of each period③.

For a five-year ordinary annuity and annuity due, each of the five equal payments (PMT) will be given as follows:

Time line for an ordinary annuity (each PMT will be given at the end of each period) is shown by Figure 2-1.

Figure 2-1　Time Line for an Ordinary Annuity

①　年金是指一定时期内每期相等金额的收付款项。

②　普通年金，也叫后付年金，是指每期期末有等额的收付款项的年金。

③　先付年金是指在一定时期内，各期期初有等额的收付款项的年金。

Time line for an annuity due (each PMT will be given at the beginning of each period) is shown by Figure 2-2.

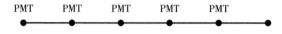

Figure 2-2　Time Line for an Annuity Due

2.2　Ordinary Annuity (后付年金)

Example: We are going to deposit $500 at the end of each year for the next five years in a bank where it will earn 6 percent interest, how much will we have at the end of five years?

Answer: As shown by Figure 2-3.

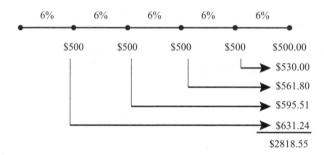

Figure 2-3　Time Line for an Ordinary Annuity with PMT of $500

$FV_5 = \$500 (1+0.06)^4 + \$500 (1+0.06)^3 + \$500 (1+0.06)^2 +$
$\quad\quad \$500 (1+0.06)^1 + \$500$
$\quad = \$2818.55$

From examining the mathematics involved and the graph of the movement of money through time we can see that this procedure can be generalized to:

$$FV_n = PMT\left[\sum_{t=0}^{n-1} (1+i)^t\right] \quad\quad\quad (2-1)$$

Where:

FV_n = the future value of the annuity at the end of the n_{th} year

PMT = the annual payment deposited or received at the end of each year

i = the annual interest (or discount) rate

n = the number of years (periods) for which the annuity will last

There is a formula that can be used to speed up this computation of (2-1). The formula is:

$$FV_n = PMT\left[\frac{(1+i)^n-1}{i}\right] \qquad (2-2)$$

Example: If you deposit $100 at the end of each year for three years in a savings account that pays 5 percent Interest per year, how much will you have at the end of three years?

Answer:

$$FV_n = PMT\left[\frac{(1+i)^n-1}{i}\right]$$

$$FV_3 = \$100\left[\frac{(1+0.05)^3-1}{0.05}\right] = \$315.25$$

Example: Calculate the FV of an ordinary annuity with a quarterly compounding (10% per year) and semiannual payments ($100) for two years.

Answer: As shown by Figure 2-4.

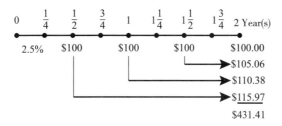

Figure 2-4   Time Line for an Ordinary Annuity with a Quarterly Compounding and Semiannual Payments

$FV = \$100 (1+0.06)^6 + \$100 (1+0.06)^4 + \$100 (1+0.06)^2 + \$100$

$\quad = \$431.41$

To aid in computing FV of annuities, the **future value interest factor for an annuity** ($FVIFA_{i,n}$)[1], defined as $\left[\sum_{t=0}^{n-1}(1+i)^{t}\right]$, is for various combinations of i and n, and its abbreviated version is shown in Table 2−1. Using this new notation, we can rewrite the equation as follows:

$$FV_n = PMT\ (FVIFA_{i,n}) \tag{2-3}$$

Reexamining Example 2, in which we determined the value after five years of $500 deposited in the bank at 6 percent, we can check the $i = 6\%$ column and $n = 5$ row in Table 2−1 and find the value of $FVIFA_{6\%,5}$ to be 5.637. Substituting this value into equation, we get:

$$FV_5 = \$500(5.637)$$
$$= \$2818.50$$

Table 2−1 $FVIFA_{i,n}$ for the Sum of an Annuity of $1 for n Years [2]

n (Period)	1%	2%	3%	4%	5%	6%	7%	8%	9%	10%
1	1.000	1.000	1.000	1.000	1.000	1.000	1.000	1.000	1.000	1.000
2	2.010	2.020	2.030	2.040	2.050	2.060	2.070	2.080	2.090	2.100
3	3.030	3.060	3.091	3.122	3.152	3.184	3.215	3.246	3.278	3.310
4	4.060	4.122	4.184	4.246	4.310	4.375	4.440	4.506	4.573	4.641
5	5.101	5.204	5.309	5.416	5.526	5.637	5.751	5.867	5.985	6.105
6	6.152	6.308	6.468	6.633	6.802	6.975	7.153	7.336	7.523	7.716
7	7.214	7.434	7.662	7.898	8.142	8.394	8.654	8.923	9.200	9.487
8	8.286	8.583	8.892	9.214	9.549	9.897	10.260	10.637	11.028	11.436
9	9.369	9.755	10.159	10.583	11.027	11.491	11.978	12.488	13.021	13.579
10	10.462	10.950	11.464	12.006	12.578	13.181	13.816	14.487	15.193	15.937

To find the PV of an ordinary annuity, we should discount the cash flows back to the present rather than compounding them forward to the terminal date of the annuity. The general formula for the PV of an ordinary annuity can be stated as:

[1]　1元年金终值系数。
[2]　1元年金终值系数表。

$$PV = PMT \left[\sum_{t=1}^{n} \frac{1}{(1 + i)^{t}} \right] \qquad (2-4)$$

or $$PV = PMT \left[\frac{1 - \dfrac{1}{(1 + i)^{n}}}{i} \right] \qquad (2-5)$$

Where:

PMT = the annual payment deposited or received at the end of each year

i = the annual interest (or discount) rate

n = the number of years for which the annuity will last

To simplify the process of determining the present value of an annuity, the present value interest factor for an annuity ($PVIFA_{i,n}$), defined as $\left[\sum_{t=1}^{n} \frac{1}{(1 + i)^{t}} \right]$, has been compiled for various combination of i and n, and its abbreviated version is provided in Table 2-2.

Table 2-2 $PVIFA_{i,n}$ for the Present Value of an Annuity of $1 for n Years [1]

n (Period)	1%	2%	3%	4%	5%	6%	7%	8%	9%	10%
1	0. 990	0. 980	0. 971	0. 962	0. 952	0. 943	0. 935	0. 926	0. 917	0. 909
2	1. 970	1. 942	1. 913	1. 886	1. 859	1. 833	1. 808	1. 783	1. 759	1. 736
3	2. 941	2. 884	2. 829	2. 775	2. 723	2. 673	2. 624	2. 577	2. 531	2. 487
4	3. 902	3. 808	3. 717	3. 630	3. 546	3. 465	3. 387	3. 312	3. 240	3. 170
5	4. 853	4. 713	4. 580	4. 452	4. 329	4. 212	4. 100	3. 993	3. 890	3. 791
6	5. 795	5. 601	5. 417	5. 242	5. 076	4. 917	4. 767	4. 623	4. 486	4. 355
7	6. 728	6. 472	6. 230	6. 002	5. 786	5. 582	5. 389	5. 206	5. 033	4. 868
8	7. 652	7. 325	7. 020	6. 733	6. 463	6. 210	5. 971	5. 747	5. 535	5. 335
9	8. 566	8. 162	7. 786	7. 435	7. 108	6. 802	6. 515	6. 247	5. 995	5. 759
10	9. 471	8. 983	8. 530	8. 111	7. 722	7. 360	7. 024	6. 710	6. 418	6. 145

[1] 1元年金现值系数表。

Using the new notation we can rewrite the equation as follows:

$$PV = PMT(PVIFA_{i,n}) \tag{2-6}$$

Example: An investor has the opportunity to purchase a financial instrument that promises to pay $500 a year for the next 10 years, beginning 1 year from now. The financial instrument is being offered for a price of $3300. The investor seeks an annual interest rate of 6% on this investment. Should the investor purchase this financial instrument?

Answer:

$$PMT = \$500$$

$$i = 6\%$$

$$n = 10$$

So, its PV is determined by $PV = PMT(PVIFA_{i,n})$, then we can look up the $i = 6\%$ column and $n = 10$ row to find the value of $PVIFA_{6\%,10}$ to be 7.360, and substitute this value into equation, then we get:

$$PV = \$500 \ (7.360)$$
$$= \$3680$$

Since the present value of an ordinary annuity of $500 per year when discounted at 6% exceeds the price of the financial instrument ($3300), this financial instrument offers an annual interest rate in excess of 6%. Therefore, it is an attractive investment for this investor.

2.3 Annuity Due (先付年金)

Because annuities due are really just ordinary annuities where all the annuity payments have been shifted forward by one year, compounding them and determining their present value is actually quite simple. Remember, with an annuity due, each annuity payment occurs at the beginning of each period rather than at the end of the period.

As you can see, in Figure 2-5 shown as follows, there are two annuities that have the same time level and payment—Just different for one is an ordinary annuity and the other is an annuity due. FV_{D1} has experienced five compounding periods while FV_{O1} has experienced four compounding periods, so $FV_{D1} = FV_{O1}(1+i)$, and FV_{D2} has experienced four compounding periods while FV_{O2} only has three, so $FV_{D2} = FV_{O2}(1+i)$, then the same goes for the relationship between every FV_{Dt} and FV_{Ot}, that is $FV_{Dt} = FV_{Ot}(1+i)$, now add them up, you will get $FV_D = FV_O(1+i)$.

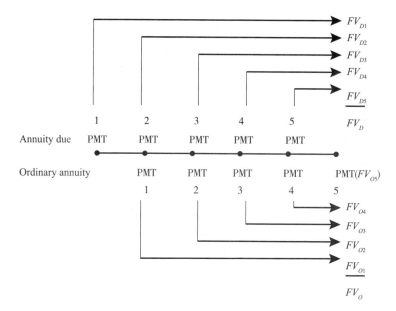

Figure 2-5   Time Line to Solve for the Future Value of Annuity Due and Ordinary Annuity

So the way to compute the future value of an annuity due (FVA_D) is to calculate the future value of an ordinary annuity (FVA_O) and simply multiply the resulting FVA_O by one plus the **periodic compounding rate** ($\dfrac{i}{m}$). Consequently, this can be expressed as:

$$FVA_D = FVA_O(1+\frac{i}{m})\qquad\qquad(2-7)$$

Example: If you deposit $100 at the beginning of each year for three years in a savings account that pays 5 percent interest per year compounded annually, how much will you have at the end of three years?

Answer:

$$FVA_D = FVA_O(1+\frac{i}{m})$$

$$= PMT(FVIFA_{i,n})(1+i/m)$$

$$= \$100(3.1525)(1+0.05/1)$$

$$= \$331.01$$

As for the PV with an annuity due, there's one less discounting period since the first cash flow occurs at $t=0$ and is already its PV. This implies that, all else being equal, the PV of an annuity due will be greater than the PV of an ordinary annuity.

As you can see, in Figure 2-6 shown as follows, there are two annuities which have the same time level and payment, one is an ordinary annuity and the other is an annuity due. PV_{D1} has experienced 0 discounting period ($PV_{D1}=\text{PMT}$) while PV_{O1} has experienced one discounting period ($PV_{O1}=\text{PMT}/(1+i)$), so $PV_{D1}=PV_{O1}(1+i)$, and PV_{D2} has experienced one compounding period ($PV_{D2}=\text{PMT}/(1+i)$) while PV_{O2} has two ($PV_{O2}=\text{PMT}/(1+i)^2$), so $PV_{D2}=PV_{O2}(1+i)$, then the same goes for the relationship between every PV_{Dt} and PV_{Ot}, that is $PV_{Dt}=PV_{Ot}(1+i)$, now add them up, you will get $PV_D=PV_O(1+i)$.

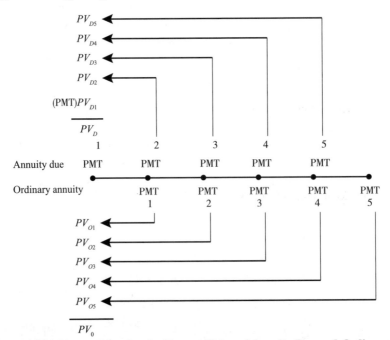

Figure 2-6　Time Line to Solve for the Present Value of Annuity Due and Ordinary Annuity

So you can treat the cash flow stream as an ordinary annuity over n compounding periods, and simply multiply the resulting PV by one plus the periodic compounding rate $(\frac{i}{m})$. Consequently, this can be expressed as:

$$PVA_D = PVA_O(1+\frac{i}{m}) \qquad (2-8)$$

Example: An investor has the opportunity to purchase a financial instrument that promises to pay \$500 a year for the next 5 years beginning now, and there is an annual interest rate of 6% on this investment. How much will the investor get at the end of 5 years?

Answer:

$$
\begin{aligned}
PVA_D &= PVA_O(1+\frac{i}{m}) \\
&= PMT(PVIFA_{i,n})(1+i/m) \\
&= \$500(4.212)(1.06) \\
&= \$2232.36
\end{aligned}
$$

2.4 Perpetuities（永续年金）

Most annuities call for payments to be made over some finite period of time. However, some annuities go on indefinitely or perpetually, and they are called perpetuities. The present value of a perpetuity is found by applying equation as follows:

$$PV = \frac{PMT}{i} \qquad (2-9)$$

Example: Suppose a company promised to pay \$100 per year in perpetuity. What would each investment instrument be worth if the opportunity cost rate was 5%?

Answer:

$$PV = \frac{\$100}{0.05} = \$2000$$

Experiment 2
Excel Implementation for Annuity

一、运用 NPV、PV 公式解决年金现值问题

例1：一个 3 期的后付年金，每期现金流为 1000 元，年利率为 8%，则该年金的现值是多少（见表 2-3）？

表 2-3　用 NPV 和 PV 函数求解资金现值

	A	B	C	D	E	F	G
19		1. 年金现值（后付年金）					
20		解法一：					
21		利率	8.00%				
22		期数	金额				
23		1	1000.00				
24		2	1000.00				
25		3	1000.00				
26		现值	2577.10	=NPV(C20,C22:C24)			
27							
28		解法二：					
29		利率	8.00%				
30		期数	3.00				
31		PMT	1000.00				
32		现值	2577.10	=PV(C29,C30,−C31, 0)			
33							
34							

后付年金，此处为0

二、运用 FV 函数或资金表的方式求解年金终值问题

例2：一个 10 年期的先付年金，每期现金流为 1000 元，利率为 10%，则 10 年末的年金终值是多少（见表 2-4）？

表 2-4　用 FV 函数或资金表求解年金终值

	I	J	K	L	M	N	O
35	2. 年金终值						
36	利率	10%		=$J$36*(J38+K38)			
37	期数	期待值	期初存入	利息	期末值	=J38+K38+L38	
38	0	0.00	1000.00	100.00	1100.00		
39	1	1100.00	1000.00	210.00	2310.00		
40	2	2310.00	1000.00	331.00	3641.00		
41	3	3641.00 =M38	1000.00	464.10	5105.10		
42	4	5105.10	1000.00	610.51	6715.61		
43	5	6715.61	1000.00	771.56	8487.17		
44	6	8487.17	1000.00	948.72	10435.89		
45	7	10435.89	1000.00	1143.59	12579.48		
46	8	12579.48	1000.00	1357.95	14937.42		
47	9	14937.42	1000.00	1593.74	17531.17		
48	10	17531.17					
49							
50		或者: =FV(J36,I48,−K38, 1)					
51							

先付年金，此处为1

Chapter 3
Amortized Loans
(分期付款)^①

Loan amortization is the process of paying off a loan with a series of periodic loan payments whereby a portion of the outstanding loan amount is paid off, or amortized, with each payment.

Example: Suppose a firm wants to purchase a piece of machinery. To do this, it borrows \$6000 to be repaid in four equal payments at the end of each of the next four years, and the interest rate that is paid to the lender is 15% on the outstanding portion of the loan. To determine what the annual payments associated with the repayment of this debt will be, we simply use equation (2-4) and solve for the value of PMT.

Answer:

$PV = \$6000$

$i = 15\%$

$n = 4$

$$PV = PMT\left[\sum_{t=1}^{n}\frac{1}{(1+i)^{t}}\right]$$

$$\$6000 = PMT\left[\sum_{t=1}^{4}\frac{1}{(1+0.15)^{t}}\right]$$

$$\$6000 = PMT\ (PVIFA_{15\%,4})$$

$$\$6000 = PMT\ (2.855)$$

$$PMT = \$2101.58$$

---

① 分期偿付的贷款。

When a company or individual enters into a long term loan, the debt is usually paid off over time with a series of equal, periodic loan payments, and each payment includes the repayment of principal and an interest charge. The amounts of the principal and interest components of the loan payment, however, does not remain fixed over the term of the loan.

Example: Construct an amortization schedule to show the interest and principal components of the end of year payments for a five-year $10000 loan with 10 percent interest rate.

Answer: As shown by Table 3-1.

Table 3-1   An Amortization Schedule for a Five-Year $10000 with 10 Percent Interest Rate ($)

Period	Beginning Balance (1)	Payment① (2)	Interest Component (3) = (1) ×10%	Principal Component (4) = (2) − (3)	Ending Balance (5) = (1) − (4)
1	10000.00	2637.97	1000.00	1637.97	8362.03
2	8362.03	2637.97	836.20	1801.77	6560.26
3	6560.26	2637.97	656.03	1981.94	4578.32
4	4578.32	2637.97	457.83	2180.14	2398.18
5	2398.18	2638.00	239.82	2398.18	0.00

---

① Use formula (2-4) to solve for the payment.

Experiment 3
Excel Implementation for Amortization

使用 PMT 函数解决分期付款问题

例：贷款总额 10000 元，年利率为 7%，在未来的 6 年里每年年末（或年初）等额还款，则年还款额是多少（见表 3-2）？

表 3-2　用 PMT 函数求解年还款额

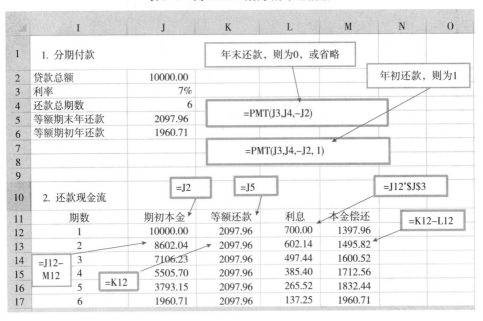

	I	J	K	L	M	N	O
1	1. 分期付款		年末还款，则为0，或省略				
2	贷款总额	10000.00			年初还款，则为1		
3	利率	7%					
4	还款总期数	6	=PMT(J3,J4,-J2)				
5	等额期末年还款	2097.96					
6	等额期初年还款	1960.71					
7			=PMT(J3,J4,-J2, 1)				
8							
9			=J2	=J5		=J12*$J$3	
10	2. 还款现金流						
11	期数	期初本金	等额还款	利息	本金偿还	=K12-L12	
12	1	10000.00	2097.96	700.00	1397.96		
13	2	8602.04	2097.96	602.14	1495.82		
14	3	7106.23	2097.96	497.44	1600.52		
15	4	5505.70	2097.96	385.40	1712.56		
16	5	3793.15	2097.96	265.52	1832.44		
17	6	1960.71	2097.96	137.25	1960.71		

（=J12-M12）（=K12）

本部分小结

一、公式小结

（1）复利计息。

一年计息一次的复利：$FV_n = PV(1+i)^n$

不完整期间（Fractional Periods）的复利：$FV_n = PV(1+i)^n$

一年多次计息的复利：$FV_n = PV\left(1+\dfrac{i}{m}\right)^{mn}$

连续复利：$FV = PV \times e^{i \times n}$

实际年利率：$EAR = \left(1+\dfrac{i}{m}\right)^m - 1$

（2）终值和现值。

公式法：$FV_n = PV\left(1+\dfrac{i}{m}\right)^{mn}$，$PV = \dfrac{FV_n}{\left(1+\dfrac{i}{m}\right)^{mn}}$

查表法：$FV_n = PV(FVIF_{i,n})$，$PV = FV_n(PVIF_{i,n})$

（3）年金。

1）后付年金终值。

公式法：$FV_n = PMT\left[\displaystyle\sum_{t=0}^{n-1}(1+i)^t\right]$，$FV_n = PMT\left[\dfrac{(1+i)^n - 1}{i}\right]$

查表法：$FV_n = PMT(FVIFA_{i,n})$

2）后付年金现值。

公式法：$PV = PMT\left[\displaystyle\sum_{t=1}^{n}\dfrac{1}{(1+i)^t}\right]$，$PV = PMT\left[\dfrac{1 - \dfrac{1}{(1+i)^n}}{i}\right]$

查表法：$PV = PMT(PVIFA_{i,n})$

先付年金终值和现值：$FVA_D = FVA_O\left(1+\dfrac{i}{m}\right)$，$PVA_D = PVA_O\left(1+\dfrac{i}{m}\right)$

永续年金现值：$PV = \dfrac{PMT}{i}$

二、难点解析

（1）复利计算时注意区别不完整期间与多次计息的应用。

例1：某银行存款利率为10%，一年计息四次，若一储户将100元存入该行，8个月后的本利和是多少？

正确答案：

$$FV_n = PV \left(1+\frac{i}{m}\right)^{mn}$$

$$= 100 \left(1+\frac{10\%}{4}\right)^{4\times\frac{8}{12}}$$

括号中的$\frac{10\%}{4}$代表一年计息4次，每个计息期间的利率为2.5%；指数部分的4代表一年计息4次，$\frac{8}{12}$代表不完整期间，即8个月是一年的$\frac{8}{12}$。

错误答案：

$$FV = 100 \left(1+\frac{10\%}{12}\right)^{8}$$

此式的含义是年利率为10%，每月计息一次，8个月后的本利和，这改变了题意中的付息方式，也就改变了实际收益率。

（2）在名义年利率相同的情况下，计息次数越多，实际年利率越大。

例2：名义年利率为10%，本金为100元。

当计息次数为 m=1 时：

当计息次数为 m=2 时：

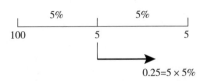

可以看出，当计息一次时，年底一次性获得10元（10%）的利息；而当计息两次时，每半年计息付息一次，所以对于100元本金来说，第一个半年，获得5元（5%）的利息，第二个半年即一年末，获得另外5元（5%）的利息。与计息一次不同的是，第一个半年获得的利息在第二个半年期间又产生了5%的利息，所以当 m=2 时，获得的总利息为5+5+0.25=10.25元。

因此，在同样的名义年利率下，计息次数越多，由利息生得的利息越多，总收益率越高。

三、Self-Test Problems 使用金融模型解决以下问题

（1）Assume that you deposit ＄1000 into asavings account that pays 8 percent.

　　a. If the bank compounds interest annually, how much will you have in your account five years from now?

　　b. If the bank compounds interest monthly, how much will you have in your account five years from now?

　　c. If the bank compounds annually, how much will you have five years and three months later?

　　d. If the bank compounds semiannually, how much will you have five years and three months later?

　　e. If the bank compounds monthly, how much will you have five years and three months later?

（2）Assume that you will need ＄1000 five years from now. Your bank compounds interest at an 8 percent annual rate.

　　a. How much should you deposit now?

　　b. If you only have ＄600 now, what interest rate, compounded annually, would you have to earn to have ＄1000 five years from now?

（3）Bank A pays 8 percent interest compoundeded semiannually, what stated annual rate should Bank B quote if Bank B compounds its interest on a monthly basis and wants to equal Bank A's effective annual rate.

（4）Mr. Brown borrows ＄4 million to buy a house, and promises a series equal payment to pay off the borrowing.

　　a. If it is to be repaid in equal installments at the end of each of the next 10 years, what is the payment per year based on a 10 percent interest rate compounded annually?

　　b. If it is to be repaid in equal installments at the end of each of the next 10 years, what is the payment per year based on a 10 percent interest rate compounded monthly?

　　c. If it is to be repaid in equal installments at the beginning of each of the next 10 years, what is the payment per year based on a 10 percent interest rate compounded annually?

    d. If he promises to pay the payment at the end of each month for 10 years, what is the payment per month based on a 10 percent interest rate compounded monthly?

    e. If he promises to pay the payment at the end of each month for 10 years, what is the payment per month based on a 10 percent interest rate compounded semiannually?

（5）A mortgage company offers to lend you $100000, and the loan calls for payments of 9221 per year for 30 years. What interest rate is the mortgage company charging you?

（6）A newly married couple has $100000 disposable income per year; they want to buy a house on a mortgage, and expect to pay off the loan in no more than 15 years. A mortgage company offers to lend them whatever they need, but charges a 10 percent interest rate compounded semiannually, so what's the maximum they could afford to borrow?

（7）You need to accumulate $200000. To do so, you plan to make deposits of $25000 per year, with the first payment being made now, in a bank account which pays 10 percent semiannual interest. Your last deposit will be less than $25000 if less is needed to save up to $200000. How many years will it take you to reach your $200000 goal, and how much will the last deposit be?

Part Two

Financing
(融资)

Chapter 4
Financing Scale
(融资规模)

Financial forecasting involves making estimates of future financing requirements of a firm. Now this chapter will give you a way to fix a firm's financing scale. Basically, forecasts of future sales revenues and associated expenses give the firm the information needed to project its future needs for financing.

The basic steps involved in predicting those financing needs are the following:

Step 1: Project the firm's sales revenues and expenses over the planning period.

Step 2: Estimate the levels of investment in current and fixed assets that are necessary to support the projected sales.

Step 3: Determine the firm's financing needs throughout the planning period.

The most commonly used method for making these projections is the percent of sales method.

The percent of sales method (销售百分比法) involves estimating the level of an expense, asset, or liability for a future period as a percent [①] of the sales forecast.

To use this method, each item in the firm's balance sheet that varies with sales is converted to a percentage of sales. The forecast of the new balance for each item is then calculated by multiplying this percentage by the projected sales for the planning period.

This method of forecasting future financing is not so precise. However, it offers a relatively low-cost and easy-to-use first approximation of the firm's financing needs for a future period.

---

① The percentage used can come from the most recent financial statement item as a percent of current sales, from an average computed over several years, from the judgment of a analyst, or from some combination of these sources.

Now, let's first see the process of the balance sheet items (see Table 4-1).

Table 4-1　Balance Sheet Items

Assets	
Current assets	Current assets are assumed to vary with the level (the same percent) of firm sales
Net fixed assets	Net fixed assets are assumed to vary with the level of firm sales when the firm does not have sufficient productive capacity to absorb a projected increase in sales
	If the fixed assets the firm currently owns were sufficient to support the projected level of new sales, then fixed assets should not be allowed to vary with sales
Total assets	The sum of current assets and net fixed assets
Liabilities and owners' equity	
Accounts payable	Accounts payable and accrued expenses are the only liabilities allowed to vary with sales. Because these two categories of current liabilities normally vary directly with the level of sales, they are often referred to as sources of spontaneous financing
Accrued expenses	
Notes payable	Notes payable, long-term debt (LTD), common stock, and paid-in capital are not assumed to vary directly with the level of firm sales. These sources of financing are termed discretionary financing
Long-term debt	
Common stock	
Retained earnings	The level of retained earnings does vary with estimated sales. The predicted change in the level of retained earnings equals the estimated after-tax profits minus the common stock dividends
Total financing provided	From all the changes of accounts payable, accrued expenses and retained earnings
Discretionary financing needed	**This part is what we wish to know**
Total	Equal to the total assets

In summary, we can estimate the firm's discretionary financing needs (DFN), using the percent of sales method of financial forecasting (see Table 4-2, Table 4-3), by following a four-step procedure:

Step 1: Convert each asset and liability account that varies directly with firm sales to a percent of the current year's sales.

Step 2: Project the level of each asset and liability account in the balance sheet using its percent of sales multiplied by projected sales or leaving the account balance unchanged where the account does not vary with the level of sales.

Step 3: Project the addition to retained earnings available to help finance the firm's operations. This equals projected net income for the period minus planned common stock dividends.

Step 4: Project the firm's discretionary financing needs as the projected level of total assets minus projected liabilities and owners' equity.

Since all these funds must be raised from sources such as bank borrowing or a new equity issue, which requires that management exercise its discretion in electing the source. We can calculate DFN using the following relationship:

$$DFN = \begin{bmatrix} \text{predicted change} \\ \text{in total assets} \end{bmatrix} - \begin{bmatrix} \text{predicted change} \\ \text{in spontaneous liabilities} \end{bmatrix} - \begin{bmatrix} \text{predicted change} \\ \text{in retained earnings} \end{bmatrix}$$

Sometimes analysts prefer to calculate a firm's external financing needs (EFN) which include all the firm's needs for financing beyond the funds provided internally through the retention of earnings. Thus,

$$EFN = \begin{bmatrix} \text{predicted change} \\ \text{in total assets} \end{bmatrix} - \begin{bmatrix} \text{predicted change} \\ \text{in retained earnings} \end{bmatrix}$$

We prefer to use the DFN concept, as it focuses the analyst's attention on the amount of funds that the firm must actively seek to meet the firm's financing requirements. For firms that have limited sources of external financing or choose to grow through internal finance plus spontaneous financing, it is important that they be able to estimate the sales growth rate that they can "afford".

Table 4-2　Using the Percent of Sales Method to Forecast
Future Financing Requirements

		Present (2018)	Percent of Sales（2018 sales=10M）	Projected (2019)（2019 sales=$12M）	
Assets	Current assets	$2.0M	$\frac{2M}{10M}=20\%$	20%×$12M = $2.4M	
	Net fixed assets	$4.0M	$\frac{4M}{10M}=40\%$	40%×$12M = $4.8M	
	Total	$6.0M		$7.2M	(Increase of assets: 7.2M－6.0M=1.2M, means total financing need is 1.2M)
Liabilities and owners' equity	Accounts payable	$1.0M	$\frac{1M}{10M}=10\%$	10%×$12M = $1.2M	Total supply: 1.2M+1.2M−1.0M−1.0M =0.4M financing
	Accrued expenses	$1.0M	$\frac{1M}{10M}=10\%$	10%×$12M = $1.2M	
	Notes payable	$0.5M	NA	No change　$0.5M	
	Long-term debt	$2.0M	NA	No change　$2.0M	
	Total liabilities	$4.5M		$4.9M	
	Common stock	$0.1M	NA	No change $0.1M	
	Paid-in capital	$0.2M	NA	No change $0.2M	
	Retained earnings	$1.2M		$1.2M+$0.27M① = $1.47M	Supply: 1.47M−1.2M =0.27M financing
	Common equity	$1.5M		1.77M	

---

① see Table 4-3.

Continued

	Present (2018)	Percent of Sales (2018 sales = 10M)	Projected (2019) (2019 sales = $ 12M)	
		Total financing provided	$ 6. 67M	
		Discretionary financing needed	$ 7. 2M – $ 6. 67M = $ 0. 53M or $ 1. 2M – $ 0. 4M – $ 0. 27M = $ 0. 53M (so this is our financing scale)	
Total $ 6. 0M			Must be the same of the assets $ 7. 2M	

Table 4–3   Income Statement

	2018	Percent of Sales	2019
Sales	$ 10M		$ 12M
Expenses	$ 9. 5M	$\frac{9.5M}{10M}=95\%$	95%× $ 12M = $ 11. 4M
Earning before tax	$ 0. 5M	$\frac{0.5M}{10M}=5\%$	5%× $ 12M = $ 0. 6M
Tax (50%)	$ 0. 25M		0. 5× $ 0. 6M = $ 0. 3M
Net income	$ 0. 25M		$ 0. 3M
Dividend (10%)	$ 0. 025M		$ 0. 03M
Retained earning	$ 0. 225M		$ 0. 27M

本章小结

一、本章要点和难点

用销售百分比法预测企业融资规模时，应注意以下几点：

（1）资产负债表的平衡。

$$资产 \quad = \quad 负债 \quad + 所有者权益$$

$$\left\{\begin{array}{c}流动资产\\+\\净固定资产\end{array}\right\} = \left\{\begin{array}{c}短期负债\\+\\长期负债\end{array}\right\} + \left\{\begin{array}{c}股本\\+\\留存收益\end{array}\right\}$$

（2）一般来说，流动资产、短期负债会随销售额等比例变化。

（3）在企业生产能力没有充分利用时，销售额的提高不会改变净固定资产的数值；而当企业生产能力已经充分利用时，销售额的提高必然是扩张生产能力的结果，因此净固定资产增大。

（4）留存收益是企业经营的历年累积和，所以预测时应在现有数值基础上加上下一年新增留存收益的预测值（由损益表各项测算）。

（5）
$$资产 \quad = \quad 负债 \quad + \quad 所有者权益$$

$$\left\{\begin{array}{c}（流动资产+A）\\+\\（净固定资产+B）\end{array}\right\} = \left\{\begin{array}{c}（短期负债+C）\\+\\长期负债\end{array}\right\} + \left\{\begin{array}{c}股本\\+\\（留存收益+D）\end{array}\right\}$$

其中，A表示与销售额等比例变化的下一年度流动资产与本年度流动资产的差值；B表示根据企业生产能力情况决定增加的固定资产值（当企业生产能力没充分使用时此项为0）；C表示与销售额等比例变化的下一年度短期负债与本年度短期负债的差值；D表示根据销售额预测的下一年度留存收益。

因此，企业融资额=A+B-C-D。

二、Self-Test Problems

4-1 FixCo. has sales of \$150 million in 2018, and predicts a sales of \$180 million in 2019. Its balance sheet and income statement in 2018 are as follows （see Table 4-4，Table 4-5）.

Table 4-4　Balance Sheet of Fixlo. in 2018 （USD in millions）

Cash	0.75
Accounts receivable	24.00
Inventory	26.10
Net fixed assets	2.95
Total assets	53.80
Accounts payable	27.45
Long-term debt	5.55
Total liabilities	33.00
Common stock	12.50
Retained earnings	8.30
Total equity	20.80
Total liabilities and shareholders' equity	53.80

Table 4-5　Income Statement of Fixlo. in 2018 （USD in millions）

Sales	150.00
Cost of goods sold	114.00
Expenses	31.50
Tax	1.80
Net income	2.70

If the fixed assets the firm currently owns were sufficient to support the projected level of new sales, what are the firm's DFN and EFN?

Chapter 5
Cost of Capital
（资本成本）

5.1 Cost of Capital（资本成本）

Most important business decisions require capital. The firm must decide how to raise the capital to fund its business or finance its growth. In order to attract new investors, companies have created a wide variety of financing instruments or securities. In this chapter we will stick to three basic types of financing instruments: debt, preferred stock, and common stock.

5.1.1 The Cost of Debt（长期债权资本成本率）

The after-tax cost of debt is the interest rate at which firms can issue new debt (r_d) net of the tax savings[①] from the tax-deductibility of interest ($r_d t$).

$$r_d(1-t)^{②} \tag{5-1}$$

Example: Somy Inc. is planning to issue new debt at an interest rate of 8 percent.

---

① 根据企业所得税法的规定，企业债务的利息允许从税前利润中扣除，从而可以抵免企业所得税。因此，企业实际负担的债权资本成本率应当考虑所得税因素。

② From the income statement in Table 4-5, we see (sales-cost-expense-interest) (1-t) = net income, that is what belongs to the stock holders, as the interest is a before tax item, if we did not pay that much, we will pay a tax for the interest, so we could only save (1-t) of the total interest. Then, the actual cost of debt is (1-t) of the nominal r_d.

Somy has a 40 percent marginal tax rate. What is Somy's cost of debt?

Answer:

$$r_d(1-t) = 8\% \ (1-40\%) = 4.8\%$$

It is important that you realize that the cost of debt is the market interest rate on new debt, not the coupon rate on the firm's existing debt.

5.1.2 The Cost of Preferred Stock（优先股资本成本率）

The cost of preferred stock (r_p) is:

$$r_p = D_p/P_{net} \tag{5-2}$$

Where:

D_p = preferred dividends（优先股每股年股利）

P_{net} = net issuing price after deducting flotation costs（优先股筹资净额，即发行价格扣除发行费用）

Example: Suppose Somy has preferred stock that pays an $10 dividend per share and sells for $100 per share. If Somy were to issue new preferred shares, it would incur a flotation cost of 5 percent. What is Somy's cost of preferred stock?

Answer:

$$r_p = D_p/P_{net}$$

$$P_{net} = 100(1-0.05) = \$95$$

$$r_p = \$10/\$95 = 0.105 = 10.5\%$$

5.1.3 The Cost of Common Stock（普通股资本成本率）

The cost of common stock can be estimated using one of the following three approaches:

(1) The Capital Asset Pricing Model Approach（CAPM，资本资产定价模型）[①]。

————————

① 资本资产定价模型的含义可以简单描述为，普通股投资的必要报酬率等于无风险报酬率加上风险报酬率。

Step 1: Estimate the risk free rate (r_f). The short-term Treasury Bill Rate is usually used as r_f.

Step 2: Estimate the stock's beta (β). This is the stock's risk measure. (If $\beta=l$, it means the stock has the same risk level as the whole market, while $\beta=a$, it means the stock has a times the risk level of the whole market.)

Step 3: Estimate the expected rate of return of the market (r_m).

Step 4: Use the capital asset pricing model (CAPM) equation to estimate the required rate of return:

$$r_s = r_f + \beta(r_m - r_f) \tag{5-3}$$

Example: Suppose r_f is 6%, r_m is 11%, and Somy has a beta of 1.1. Please use CAPM to estimate r_s.

Answer:

$$r_s = 6\% + 1.1(11\% - 6\%) = 11.5\%$$

(2) Bond Yield Plus Risk Premium Approach (债券投资报酬率加股票投资风险报酬率)。

Analysts often add a risk premium (3 to 5 percentage points) to the interest rate of the firm's long-term debt to estimate the required rate of return. [①]

$$r_s = \text{bond yield} + \text{risk premium} \tag{5-4}$$

Example: Somy's interest rate on long term debt is 8 percent. Suppose the risk premium is estimated to be 5 percent. What's Somy's cost of equity?

Answer:

$$r_s = 8\% + 5\% = 13\%$$

(3) The Discounted Cash Flow or Dividend-Yield-Plus-Growth-Rate Approach (股利折现模型)。

If dividends are expected to grow at a constant rate 'g', then the current price of the stock is given by the dividend growth model:

$$P_0 = \frac{D_1}{r_s - g}$$

----

① 从投资者的角度，股票投资的风险高于债券，因此股票投资的必要报酬率可以在债券利率的基础上再加股票投资高于债券投资的风险报酬率。

Where:

D_1 = next year's dividend

r_s = the investor's required rate of return

g = the firm's expected constant growth rate

Rearranging the terms you can solve for r_s:

$$r_s = \frac{D_1}{P_0} + g \tag{5-5}$$

In order to use $r_s = \frac{D_1}{P_0} + g$, you have to estimate the expected growth rate 'g'. This can be done by using the growth rate projected by security analysts or through the following equation:

$$g = (\text{retention rate})(\text{return on equity})$$
$$= (1 - \text{payout rate})(\text{ROE})$$

Example: Suppose Somy's stock sells for \$21.00, next year's dividend is expected to be \$1.00, Somy's expected ROE is 12 percent, and Somy is expected to pay out 40 percent of its earnings. What is Somy's cost of equity?

Answer:

$$g = (\text{retention rate})(\text{ROE})$$
$$= (1 - 0.4)(0.12)$$
$$= 0.072 = 7.2\%$$
$$r_s = (1/21) + 0.072 = 0.12 = 12\%$$

5.1.4 The Cost of Newly Issued Common Stock (新股成本)

The cost of new common stock (r_e) will be higher than the cost of existing stock because of the existence of flotation costs. Cost of new common equity is given by:

$$r_e = \frac{D_1}{P_0(1-F)} + g \tag{5-6}$$

Where:

f = the percentage flotation cost incurred in selling new stock

= (current stock price−funds going to company) / current stock price

Example: Somy's stock sells for $21.00, next year's dividend is expected to be $1, Somy's expected ROE is 12 percent, and Somy is expected to pay out 40 percent of its earnings. Now, assume that Somy has a flotation cost of 10 percent and calculate the cost of new stock.

Answer: The cost of new equity for Somy is:

$$g = (1-0.4)(0.12) = 0.072$$

$$r_e = \frac{1}{21(1-0.1)} + 0.072 = 0.125 \text{ or } 12.5\%$$

5.1.5 The Weighted Avergae Capital Cost (综合资本成本率)

If a company successfully funds its capital by a variety of financing instruments, the weighted average cost of per $1 it funds will be the weighted average capital cost (WACC, 综合资本成本率①).

The WACC is given by:

$$WACC = (w_d)[r_d(1-t)] + (w_p)(r_p) + (w_s)(r_s) \tag{5-7}$$

Where:

w_d = the percentage of debt in the capital structure

w_p = the percentage of preferred stock in the capital structure

w_s = the percentage of common stock in the capital structure

As indicated above, these weights are based on the market value of the firm's securities.

Example: Suppose Somy's target capital structure is as follows:

$$w_d = 0.45, \ w_p = 0.05, \ w_s = 0.50, \ t = 0.4$$

$$\text{and } r_d = 8\%, \ r_p = 8.4\%, \ r_s = 12.5\%$$

Please calculate Somy's WACC.

---

① 综合资本成本率是指一个企业全部长期资本的成本率，通常是以各种长期资本的比例为权重，对个别资本成本率进行加权平均测算的，故亦称加权平均资本成本率。

Answer:

$$WACC = (0.45)[(0.08)(1-0.4)]+(0.05)(0.084)+(0.50)(0.125)$$
$$= 0.0883 = 8.83\%$$

5.2 Optimal Capital Structure (最优资本结构)

5.2.1 Beta Coefficient

An increase in the debt ratio will not only increase the cost of debt, but also increase the risk faced by share holders, and this has an effect on the cost of equity, r_s. That is to say, beta increases with financial leverage. The following equation is to specify the effect of financial leverage on beta:

$$\beta = \beta_u [1+(1-t)(\frac{D}{S})] \qquad (5-8)$$

The equation shows how increases in the market value debt-equity ratio increase beta. Here β_u is the firm's un-leveraged beta coefficient, that is, the beta the firm would have if it has no debt.

As a starting point, a firm can use its current beta, tax rate, and debt-equity ratio to calculate its un-leveraged beta, by simply transforming above equation as follows:

$$\beta_u = \beta / [1+(1-t)(\frac{D}{S})] \qquad (5-9)$$

Then, once β_u is determined, the equation can be used to estimate how changes in the debt-equation ratio would affect the leveraged beta. And use equation (5-3) we can get the cost of equity r_s.

Example: Somy Inc. is considering a large-scale recapitalization. Currently, Somy is financed with 25 percent debt and 75 percent equity. Somy is considering increasing its level of debt until it is financed with 60 percent debt and 40 percent equity. The beta on its common stock at the current level of debt is 1.5, the risk free rate is 6 percent, the market risk premium is 4 percent, and Somy faces a 40 percent tax rate.

(1) What is Somy's current cost of equity?

Answer:

$$r_s = 6\% + 1.5(4\%) = 12\%$$

(2) What isSomy's unevered beta?

Answer:

$$\beta_u = 1.5/[1+(1-0.4)(25/75)] = 1.25$$

(3) What will be the new betaand new cost of equity if Somy recapitalizes?

Answer:

$$\beta = 1.25[1+(1-0.4)(60/40)] = 2.375$$
$$r_s' = 6\% + (2.375)(4\%) = 15.5\%$$

5.2.2 Estimating a Firm's Value

The value of a firm is the present value of its expected future net income (NI) discounted at its WACC:

$$V = \sum_{t=1}^{\infty} \frac{NI_t}{(1 + WACC)^t} \tag{5-10}$$

Or the sum of the value of its debt and equity:

$$V = D + S \tag{5-11}$$

If the company has zero growth ($g=0$) or a constant growth, we can use the constant growth version of the equation:

$$V = \frac{NI_0(1+g)}{WACC-g} \tag{5-12}$$

Notice that the firm's maximum value occurs at a capital structure that minimizes the WACC.

5.2.3 Estimating Shareholder Wealth and Stock Price

When the capital structure is adjusted to a larger leverage, the firm should recapitalize, meaning that it should issue debt and use the proceeds to repurchase stock.

The shareholder's wealth after the recap, as it is commonly called, would be equal to the payment they receive from the share repurchase plus the remaining value of their equity.

To find the remaining value of equity, we need to specify how much debt is issued in the new capital structure. Since we know the percent of debt in the capital structure and the resulting value of the firm, we can find the dollar value of debt as follows:

$$D = w_d V \qquad (5-13)$$

The market value of the remaining equity S, is equal to the total value minus the value of the debt.

Notice that the value of equity declines as the percent financed with debt increases. But keep in mind that the shareholders will receive cash equal to the amount of new debt when the company repurchases the stock (cash raised by issuing debt, $\Delta D = D - D_0$).

Here D_0 is the amount of debt the company had before the recap, thus the total wealth of the shareholders after the repurchase will be the cash they receive in the repurchase plus the value of their remaining equity.

The post-repurchase price per share is:

$$P_1 = [S_1 + (D_1 - D_0)]/n_0 \qquad (5-14)$$

The number of remaining shares after the repurchase, n, is

$$n_1 = n_0 - (\Delta D/P_1) \qquad (5-15)$$

Example: Somy Inc. is currently in this situation: ①EBIT = \$4.7 million; ②tax rate, $t = 40\%$; ③value of debt, $D = \$2$ million; ④$r_d = 10\%$, $r_s = 15\%$; ⑤shares of stock outstanding, $n_0 = 600000$; and stock price, $P_0 = \$30$.

The firm's market is stable, and it expects no growth, so all earnings are paid out as dividends. The debt consists of perpetual bonds. Suppose the firm can increase its debt so that its capital structure has 50 percent debt based on market values. At this level of debt, its cost of equity rises to 18.5 percent. Its interest rate on all debt will rise to 12 percent.

What is the stock price after the repurchase and how many shares will remain outstanding after the repurchase?

Answer:

Since new $WACC = (0.5)[(12\%)(1-0.4)] + (0.5)(18.5\%)$

$\qquad\qquad = 12.85\%$

$$g = 0, NI = EBIT(1-t) = \$4700000(0.6)$$
$$V_1 = NI/WACC = \$4700000(0.6)/0.1285$$
$$= \$21945525.292$$
$$D_1 = w_d V_1 = 0.5(\$21945525.292)$$
$$= \$10972762.646.$$

Since it started with \$2 million debt, it will issue:

$$\Delta D = D_1 - D_0 = \$10972762.646 - \$2000000$$
$$= \$8972762.646$$
$$S_1 = V_1 - D_1 = \$10972762.646$$
$$P_1 = [S_1 + (D_1 - D_0)]/n_0$$
$$= (\$10972762.646 + \$8972762.646)/600000$$
$$= \$33.243$$

It used the proceeds of the new debt, \$8972762.646 to repurchase x shares of stock at a price of \$33.243 per share. The number of shares it will repurchase is:

$$x = \$8972762.646/\$33.243 = 269914$$

Therefore, there are $600000 - 269914 = 330086$ remained.

5.2.4 The Marginal Cost of Capital and Break Point

The marginal cost of capital (MCC, 边际资本成本率) is the cost of one more dollar of capital. The MCC increases as a firm increases the amount of capital it raises during a given period. You can see that as long as a company keeps its capital structure on target for each dollar it raises (by issuing debt and preferred stock and retaining earnings), the cost of capital will be WACC.

However, at some point the firm's retained earnings will be exhausted. Beyond that point, the company will need to issue new common stock and its cost of capital will increase. The cost of debt may increase when larger amounts of capital are raised as well. Larger amounts of borrowing means riskier debt is being issued, so the required rate of return is higher.

The break point (BP, 筹资总额分界点) on the marginal cost curve is given by:

Retained earnings break point or $BP_{RE} = \dfrac{retained\ earnings}{w_s}$ (5-16)

Example: Suppose Somy Inc. estimates its earnings to be $100 million next year and has a payout ratio of 40 percent. What's Somy's retained earnings break point and what does it mean?

Retained earnings for next year will be:

Answer: $RE = \$100$ million $(1-0.4) = \$60$ million

The break point will be:

$BP_{RE} = \$60$ million $/0.5 = \$120$ million

This means after Somy has raised total capital of $120 million, the firm will be forced to issue new common stock and Somy's WACC will jump.

Experiment 4
Excel Implementation for WACC

用 Excel 解决 WACC 问题

例：已知 risk-free rate 为 3%，market risk premium 为 10.4%，已知 4 家公司的股权价值、债权价值、beta 值，求各公司的 WACC（使用 CAPM 模型计算股权成本，见表 5-1）。

表 5-1　用 CAPM 模型求解 WACC

	A	B	C	D	E	F	G	H	I	J
1										
2		Market risk premium	10.40%					=$C$3+$C$2*E6		
3		Risk-free rate	3%							
4										
5			Market Equity	Debt	Equity Beta	Cost of Debt	Marginal Tax Rate	Cost of Equity	WACC	
6	firm 1		10240000.00	2000000.00	1.5	6.80%	35.00%	18.60%	16.28%	
7	firm 2		103000000.00	50000000.00	2.1	7.30%	40.00%	24.84%	18.15%	
8	firm 3		18900000.00	0.00	1.9	4.00%	32.00%	22.76%	22.76%	
9	firm 4		289000000.00	776820000.00	3.2	8.10%	35.00%	36.28%	13.67%	
10										
11										
12								=H6*(C6/(C6+D6))+F6*(1−G6)*		
13								(D6/(D6+C6))		
14										
15										

本章小结

一、本章主要公式

（1）融资成本。

长期债权资本成本率：$r_d(1-t)$

优先股资本成本率：$r_p = D_p / P_{net}$

普通股资本成本率：①资本资产定价模型：$r_s = r_f + \beta(r_m - r_f)$

②债券投资报酬率加股票风险报酬率：$r_s = $ bond yield + risk premium

③股利折现模型：$r_s = \dfrac{D_1}{P_0} + g$

（2）综合资本成本率：$WACC = (w_d)[r_d(1-t)] + (w_p)(r_p) + (w_s)(r_s)$

（3）最优资本结构：不同资本结构的 $\dfrac{D}{S}$ 决定 β，$\beta = \beta_u[1 + (1-t)(\dfrac{D}{S})]$，$\beta$ 决定 r_s，$r_s = r_f + \beta(r_m - r_f)$，$r_s$ 进一步决定 $WACC$，$WACC = (w_d)[r_d(1-t)] + (w_p)(r_p) + (w_s)(r_s)$，$WACC$ 最小时的 $\dfrac{D}{S}$ 为最优资本结构。

（4）在调整资本结构（尤其是增加债权、减少股权）时，会进行债权融资替换股权（回购赎买流通中的股票），因此资本结构调整后的股票价格和数量都会发生变化。我们可以通过以下公式求出资本结构调整后的股票价格。

$$V_0 = \frac{NI}{WACC_0} \text{ (the same } NI) \quad \frac{NI}{WACC_1} = V_1$$

$$\left\{ \begin{array}{c} W_{d_0} \times V_0 = D_0 \\ + \\ W_{s_0} \times V_0 = S_0 \end{array} \right\} \qquad \left\{ \begin{array}{c} D_1 = W_{d_1} \times V_1 \\ + \\ S_1 = W_{s_1} \times V_1 \end{array} \right\}$$

第一步，债权融资为 $\Delta D = D_1 - D_0$。

第二步，新增债权将全部用于回赎股票（但此时还未实施回赎行为），股票价格由 P_0 变为 P_1，且一直持续下去。此时股票总价值为 $P_1 \times n_0$。

第三步，按新的股票价格 P_1 回赎 Δn 股股票，市场上股票数量由原来的 n_0 变为资本结构调整完毕后的 n_1。也就是说原有的 n_0 股分为了两部分，一部分 Δn 被新增债权融资购买，另一部分继续留在市场上为 n_1，即 $(n_0 = \Delta n + n_1)$。

从价值来看，由于第二步中股价已变为 P_1 且一直持续下去，所以 $P_1 n_0 = P_1 \Delta n + P_1 n_1$，$P_1 \Delta n$ 部分即回赎股票总值等于 ΔD，$P_1 n_1$ 即现有股票总市值等于 S_1。因此我们也可把 $P_1 n_0 = P_1 \Delta n + P_1 n_1$ 写为 $P_1 n_0 = \Delta D + S_1$，即可求出 $P_1 = \dfrac{\Delta D + S_1}{n_0}$。

二、Self-Test Problems

5-1 The ABC Company is currently in this situation: ① EBIT = \$ 4.7 million; ② tax rate, T = 40%; ③ value of debt, D = \$ 2 million; ④ r_d = 10%; ⑤ r_s = 15%; ⑥ shares of stock outstanding, n_0 = 600000; and stock price, P_0 = \$ 30. The firm's market is stable, and it expects no growth, so all earnings are paid out as dividends. The debt consists of perpetual bonds.

a. what is the total market value of the firm's stock, S, and the firm's total market value, V?

b. what is the firm's weighted average cost of capital?

c. suppose the firm can increase its debt so that its capital structure has 50 percent debt based on market values (it will issue debt and buy back stock). At this level of debt, its cost of equity rises to 18.5 percent. Its interest rate on all debt will rise to 12 percent (it will have to call and refund the old debt). What is the WACC under this capital structure? What is the total value? How much debt will it issue, and what is the stock price after the repurchase? How many shares will remain outstanding after the repurchase?

5-2 Tomy Industrial Corporation (TIC) is considering a large-scale recapitalization. Currently, TIC is financed with 25 percent debt and 75 percent equity. TIC is considering increasing its level of debt until it is financed with 50 percent debt and 50 percent equity. The beta on its common stock at the current level of debt is 1.4, the risk free rate is 6 percent, the market risk premium is 5 percent, and TIC faces a 40 percent tax rate.

a. what is TIC's current cost of equity?

b. what is TIC's unlevered beta?

c. what will be the new beta and new cost of equity if TIC recapitalizes?

5-3 Olymic Athletics is trying to determine its optimal capital structure which now consists of only debt and common equity. The firm does not currently use preferred stock in its capital structure, and it does not plan to do so in the future. To estimate how much its debt would cost at different debt levels, the company's treasury staff has consulted with investment bankers and, on the basis of those discussions, has created Table 5-2:

Table 5-2　Data to Determine Optimal Capital Structure

Market Debt-to-value ratio (w_d)	Bond rating	Before-tax cost of debt (r_d,%)
0.0	A	7.0
0.2	BBB	8.0
0.4	BB	10.0
0.6	C	12.0
0.8	D	15.0

Use the CAPM to estimate its cost of common equity, r_s. The company estimates that the risk free rate is 5 percent, the market risk premium is 6 percent, and its tax rate is 40 percent. Olymic estimates that if it had no debt, its "unlevered" beta would be 1.2. Based on this information, what is the firm's optimal capital structure, and what would the weighted average cost of capital be at the optimal capital structure?

Part Three

Investment
(投资)

Chapter 6
Risk and Return
（风险与收益）

One of the most important concepts in finance deals with risk and return. In this chapter, we start from the basic premise that investors like return and dislike risk.

To begin our study, we will define expected return and risk and offer suggestions as to how the important concept of return and risk can be measured quantitatively. We also compare the historical relationship between risk and rates of return. We will then explain how diverse investments can affect the expected return and risk of those investments. We also consider how the risk of an investment should affect the required rate of return on an investment.

Here, risk refers to the chance that some unfavorable event will occur. Investment risk, then, is related to the probability of actually earning a low or negative return—The greater the chance of a low or negative return, the riskier the investment.

No investments should be undertaken unless the expected rate of return is high enough to compensate the investor for the perceived risk of the investment.

6.1   Measurement of Return （收益度量）

6.1.1   Probability Distributions（概率分布）

An event's probability is defined as the chance that the event will occur. If all possible events are listed, and a probability is assigned to each event, the listing is called a probability distribution.

Probabilities can also be assigned to the possible outcomes from an investment. Assume you purchase a stock of a company. Looking at the past returns of the firm's stock, the rate of return probability distributions for the stock is shown in Table 6-1.

Table 6-1　Probability Distributions of a Stock

Chance of occurrence (%)	Rate of return on investment (%)
10	0
20	5
40	10
20	15
10	20

Investing in the company could conceivably provide a return as high as 20 percent if all goes well, or no return (0 percent) if everything goes against the firm. So in future years, both good and bad, we could expect a 10 percent return on average.

$$\bar{r} = (0.10)(0\%)+(0.20)(5\%)+(0.40)(10\%)+(0.20)(15\%)+(0.10)(20\%)$$
$$= 10\%$$

6.1.2　Expected Rate of Return (期望收益率)

If we multiply each possible outcome by its probability of occurrence and then sum these products, we have a weighted average of outcomes. The weights are the probabilities, and the weighted average is the expected rate of return, $\bar{r}$, called "r-hat". The expected rate of return from expected data for a single risky asset can be calculated as:

$$E(R) = \sum_{i=1}^{n} P_i R_i = P_1 R_1 + P_2 R_2 + \cdots + P_n R_n \tag{6-1}$$

Where:

P_i = probability that state i will occur

R_i = asset return if the economy is in state i

The expected return, based on expected data, is simply the weighted mean of the distribution of all possible returns.

The expected rate of return from historical data for a single risky asset can be calculated as:

$$E(R) = \bar{R} = \frac{\sum_{t=1}^{n} R_t}{n} = \frac{(R_1 + R_2 + \cdots + R_n)}{n} \qquad (6-2)$$

Where:

R_t = the return in time period t

n = the number of time periods (using historical returns)

Example: The first three columns of Table 6-2 contain the probability of outcomes and the returns for a security in each state of the economy. Calculate the expected return on the security.

Answer: The computation of expected return is illustrated in the fourth column of Table 6-2.

Table 6-2   Computing Expected Return

State	Probability (P_i)	Return (R_i)	Expected return (P_iR_i)
Expansion	0.25	5.0%	(0.25)(5.0%)= 1.25%
Normal	0.50	10.0%	(0.50)(10.0%)= 5.00%
Recession	0.25	15.0%	(0.25)(15.0%)= 3.75%

$$E(R) = \sum_{i=1}^{3} P_iR_i = 10.00\%$$

Example: Assume that the returns on a stock over the first six months of the year are +10%, -15%, +20%, +25%, -30%, and +20%. Compute the expected return.

Answer:

$$\bar{R} = \frac{0.10-0.15+0.20+0.25-0.30+0.20}{6} = 0.05 = 5.0\%$$

6.2 Risk Measurement (风险度量)

6.2.1 Variance and Standard Deviation (方差和标准差)

In finance, the variance and standard deviation of expected returns are common measures of investment risk. Both of these related measures determine the variability of a distribution of returns about its mean.

The variance and standard deviation of rates of return from expected data for an individual investment are calculated as:

$$\text{Variance} = \sigma^2 = \sum_{i=1}^{n} P_i \left[R_i - E(R) \right]^2 \qquad (6-3)$$

$$\text{Standard deviation} = \sigma = \sqrt{\sigma^2} \qquad (6-4)$$

Where:

R_i = rate of return in state i

P_i = probability of state i occurring

$E(R)$ = expected return

Thus, the standard deviation is essentially a weighted average of the deviations from the expected value, and it provides an idea of how far above or below the expected value the actual value is likely to be.

Example: Using the expected data in Table 6-2, calculate the variance and standard deviation of expected returns in Table 6-3. (Recall from the previous example that the expected return is 10 percent.)

Table 6-3 Computing the Varianle and Standard Deviation

State	Probability (P_i)	Return (R_i)	$E(R)$	$[(R_i)-E(R)]^2$	$P_i[(R_i)-E(R)]^2$
Expansion	0.25	5.0%	0.10	0.0025	(0.25)(0.0025) = 0.000625

Continued

State	Probability (P_i)	Return (R_i)	$E(R)$	$[(R_i)-E(R)]^2$	$P_i[(R_i)-E(R)]^2$
Normal	0.50	10.0%	0.10	0.0000	(0.50) (0.0000) = 0.000000
Recession	0.25	15.0%	0.10	0.0025	(0.25) (0.0025) = 0.000625

$$\text{Variance} = \sigma^2 = \sum_{i=1}^{3} P_i[R_i - E(R)]^2 = 0.000625 + 0.000000 + 0.000625 = 0.00125$$

$$\text{Standard deviation} = \sqrt{0.00125} = 0.0354 = 3.54\%$$

In the previous example, we described the procedure for finding the mean and standard deviation when the data are in the form of a known probability distribution. If only sample returns data over some past period are available, the standard deviation of returns can be estimated using this formula:

$$\text{Estimated } \sigma = S = \sqrt{\frac{\sum_{t=1}^{n} (r_t - \bar{r})^2}{n-1}} \tag{6-5}$$

Here r_t denotes the past realized rate of return in period t, and $\bar{r}$ is the average annual return earned during the last n years.

Example: Using the data in Table 6-4, calculate the mean and estimate the standard deviation.

Table 6-4   Rate of Return in 2005-2007

Year	r_t
2005	15%
2006	-5%
2007	20%

Answer:

$$\bar{r} = \frac{(15-5+20)\%}{3} = 10.0\%$$

$$\text{Estimated } \sigma = \sqrt{\frac{(15\%-10\%)^2+(-5\%-10\%)^2+(20\%-10\%)^2}{3-1}}$$

$$= 13.23\%$$

Because past variability is likely to be repeated, the historical σ is often used as an estimate of the future σ.

6.2.2 The Coefficient of Variation (标准离差率)

If a choice has to be made between two investments that have the same expected returns but different standard deviations, most people would choose the one with the lower standard deviation and, therefore, the lower risk.

Similarly, given two investments with the same risk (standard deviation) but different expected returns, investors would generally prefer the investment with the higher expected return. To most people, this is common sense—return is "good", risk is "bad", and consequently investors want as much return and as little risk as possible.

But how do we choose between two investments if one has the higher expected return but the other the lower standard deviation? To help answer this question, we often use another measure of risk, the coefficient of variation (CV), which is the standard deviation divided by the expected return:

$$\text{Coefficient of variation} = CV = \frac{\sigma}{\hat{r}} \qquad (6-6)$$

The coefficient of variation shows the risk per unit of return, and it provides a more meaningful basis for comparison when the expected returns on two alternatives are not the same.

For a case where the coefficient of variation is necessary, consider projects X and Y. These projects have different expected rates of return and different standard deviations. Project X has a 60 percent expected rate of return and a 15 percent standard deviation, while project Y has an 8 percent expected return but only a 3 percent standard deviation. Is project X riskier, on a relative basis, because it has the larger standard deviation? If we calculate the coefficient of variation of project X, we get $15/60 = 0.25$, while project Y has a coefficient of variation of $3/8 = 0.375$. Thus, we see that project

Y actually has higher risk per unit of return than project X, in spite of the fact that X's standard deviation is larger.

Therefore, even though project Y has a lower standard deviation, according to the coefficient of variation it is riskier than project X.

6.3　Risk and Return in a Portfolio Context (资产组合的风险收益)

In the preceding section we considered the risk and return of assets held in isolation. Now we analyze the risk and return of assets held in portfolios (资产组合).

6.3.1　Expected Return for a Portfolio of Risky Assets

The expected return on a portfolio of assets is simply the weighted average of the returns on the individual assets weighted by their portfolio weights. Thus, for a portfolio, the expected return is:

$$E(R_p) = \sum_{i=1}^{n} w_i E(R_i) = w_1 E(R_1) + w_2 E(R_2) + \cdots + w_n E(R_n) \qquad (6-7)$$

Where:

$E(R_i)$ = expected return on asset i

w_i = percentage of the total portfolio value invested in asset i

Example: Assume that in August 2007, a security analyst estimated that the following returns could be expected on the stocks of four large companies (see Table 6-5):

Table 6-5　Four Companies' Expected Return

	Expected return, $\hat{r}$
Microsoft	12.0%
GE	11.5

	Continued
	Expected return, $\hat{r}$
IBM	10. 0
Coca-Cola	9. 5

Answer: If we formed a $ 100000 portfolio, investing $ 25000 in each stock, the expected portfolio return would be 10. 75 percent:

$$E(R) = w_1 E(R_1) + w_2 E(R_2) + w_3 E(R_3) + w_4 E(R_4)$$
$$= 0.25(12\%) + 0.25(11.5\%) + 0.25(10.0\%) + 0.25(9.5\%)$$
$$= 10.75\%$$

6.3.2 Portfolio Risk Measurement

As we just saw, the expected return on a portfolio is simply the weighted average of the expected returns on the individual assets in the portfolio. However, unlike returns, the risk of a portfolio, σ_p, is generally not the weighted average of the standard deviations of the individual assets in the portfolio. In fact, it is theoretically possible to combine stocks that are individually quite risky as measured by their standard deviations to form a portfolio that is completely risk-less with $\sigma_p = 0$.

The reason two stocks A and B can be combined to form a risk-less portfolio is that their returns move counter cyclically to each other: when A's returns fall, those of B rise, and vice versa. The tendency of two variables to move together is called correlation, and the correlation coefficient measures this tendency. But firstly, we should to know about the covariance.

6.3.3 Covariance (协方差)

Covariance measures the extent to which two variables move together over time. A positive covariance means that the variables tend to move together. A negative covariance means that the two variables tend to move in opposite directions. A covariance of zero means there is no relationship between the two variables.

The covariance between two assets computed from expected data is equal to:

$$\text{Cov}_{1,\,2} = \sum_{i=1}^{n} \{ P_i [R_{i,\,1} - E(R_1)] \, [R_{i,\,2} - E(R_2)] \} \qquad (6\text{-}8)$$

Where:

$R_{i,1}$ = return on asset 1 in state i

$R_{i,2}$ = return on asset 2 in state i

P_i = probability of state i occurring

$E(R_1)$ = expected return on asset 1

$E(R_2)$ = expected return on asset 2

Example: Calculate the covariance between asset 1 and asset 2 with the returns distribution described in the first three columns of Table 6-6.

Answer: First, we must compute the expected return for each of the assets as follows:

$$E(R_1) = \sum_{i=1}^{n} P_i R_{i,\,1} = 0.25\ (0.05)\ +0.50\ (0.15)\ +0.25\ (0.25)$$

$$= 0.0125 + 0.0750 + 0.0625$$

$$= 0.15$$

$$E(R_2) = \sum_{i=1}^{n} P_i R_{i,\,2} = 0.25\ (0.32)\ +0.50\ (0.14)\ +0.25\ (0.04)$$

$$= 0.08 + 0.07 + 0.01$$

$$= 0.16$$

Then we can compute the covariance following the procedure illustrated in Table 6-6.

Table 6-6   Computing Covariance

P_i	$R_{i,1}$	$R_{i,2}$	$(R_{i,\,1}) - E(R_1)$	$(R_{i,\,2}) - E(R_2)$	$P_i\,[R_{i,\,1} - E(R_1)]\,[R_{i,\,2} - E(R_2)]$
0.25	0.05	0.32	−0.10	+0.16	−0.004
0.50	0.15	0.14	+0.00	−0.02	0.000
0.25	0.25	0.04	+0.10	−0.12	−0.003

$$\text{Cov}_{1,\,2} = \sum_{i=1}^{n} \{ P_i [R_{i,\,1} - E(R_1)] \, [R_{i,\,2} - E(R_2)] \} = -0.007$$

The covariance between two asset returns using historical data is computed as:

$$Cov_{1,2} = \frac{\sum_{i=1}^{n} \{ [R_{t,1} - \overline{R}_1] [R_{t,2} - \overline{R}_2] \}}{n} \qquad (6-9)$$

Where:

$R_{t,1}$ = return on asset 1 in period t

$R_{t,2}$ = return on asset 2 in period t

n = number of returns

$\overline{R}_1$ = mean return on asset 1

$\overline{R}_2$ = mean return on asset 2

Example: Calculate the covariance for the returns of stock 1 and stock 2 given the six years of historical returns in the first three columns of Table 6-7.

Answer: The covariance calculation is demonstrated in the right side of Table 6-7.

Table 6-7   Calculating Covariance from Historical Returns

Year	Stock 1	Stock 2	$(R_t - \overline{R}_1)$	$(R_t - \overline{R}_2)$	$(R_t - \overline{R}_1)(R_t - \overline{R}_2)$
2001	+0.10	+0.20	+0.05	+0.10	+0.005
2002	-0.15	-0.20	-0.20	-0.30	+0.060
2003	+0.20	-0.10	+0.15	-0.20	-0.030
2004	+0.25	+0.30	+0.20	+0.20	+0.040
2005	-0.30	-0.20	-0.35	-0.30	+0.105
2006	+0.20	+0.60	+0.15	+0.50	+0.075
	$\overline{R}_1 = 0.05$	$\overline{R}_2 = 0.10$			$\sum = 0.255$ $Cov_{1,2} = 0.255/6 = 0.0425$

6.3.4　Correlation (相关系数)

Covariance can be standardized by dividing by the product of the standard deviations of the two securities being compared. This standardized measure of co-movement is called correlation and is computed as:

$$\rho_{1,2} = \frac{\mathrm{Cov}_{1,2}}{\sigma_1 \sigma_2} \qquad (6-10)$$

The symbol for the correlation coefficient is the Greek letter rho, ρ. In statistical terms, we say that the returns on stocks A and B are perfectly negatively correlated with $\rho = -1.0$. The opposite of perfect negative correlation, is perfect positive correlation, with $\rho = +1.0$ returns on two perfectly positively correlated stocks would move up and down together, and a portfolio consisting of two such stocks would be exactly as risky as each individual stock.

　　Example: The covariance between the returns on two stocks is 0.0425. The standard deviations of stocks 1 and 2 are 0.2041 and 0.2944, respectively.

　　Calculate and interpret the covariance between the two assets.

Answer:

$$\rho_{1,2} = \frac{0.0425}{0.2041 \times 0.2944} = 0.71$$

The returns from the two stocks are positively correlate, meaning they tend to move in the same direction at the sametime. However, the correlation is not perfect because the correlation coefficient is less than one.

　　Earlier we showed that the expected return of a portfolio is the weighted average of the expected returns of the individual assets in the portfolio. This is not the case for the variance and standard deviation of a portfolio of risky assets.

　　Portfolio variance is not only a function of the variance of the returns of the individual assets in the portfolio. It is also a function of the correlation among the returns of the assets in the portfolio.

　　The general formula for the standard deviation for a portfolio of n risky assets is as follows:

$$\sigma_p = \sqrt{\sigma_p^2} = \sqrt{\sum_i^n w_i^2 \sigma_i^2 + \sum_{i=1}^n \sum_{j=1}^n w_i w_j \mathrm{Cov}_{i,j}} \qquad (i \neq j) \qquad (6-11)$$

Where:

σ_p^2 = portfolio variance

w_i = the market weight of asset i

σ_i^2 = variance of returns of assets

$\mathrm{Cov}_{i,j}$ = the covariance between the returns of assets i and j

For a portfolio of two risky assets we have:

$$\sigma_p = \sqrt{w_1^2 \sigma_1^2 + w_2^2 \sigma_2^2 + 2 w_1 w_2 \sigma_1 \sigma_2 \rho_{1,2}} \qquad (6-12)$$

Note that in the formula for a two-asset portfolio we have substituted $\sigma_1 \sigma_2 \rho_{1,2}$ for $\mathrm{Cov}_{1,2}$ because the formula is often written in this way as well to emphasize the role of correlation in portfolio.

The first part of the formula is the risk of individual assets in the portfolio. The second part of the formula is there because the risk of a portfolio of risky assets also depends on how the returns on the assets move in relation to each other.

Note that if the asset returns are negatively correlated, the final term in the formula for a two-asset portfolio is negative and reduces the portfolio standard deviation.

If the correlation is zero, the final term is zero, and the portfolio standard deviation is greater than that of a portfolio when the correlation is negative.

If the correlation is positive, the final term is positive, and portfolio standard deviation is still greater. The maximum standard deviation for a portfolio of two assets with given weights will be resulted, when the correlation coefficient is +1. When assets are perfectly positively correlated, there is no diversification benefit.

When stocks are perfectly negatively correlated, all risk can be diversified away, but when stocks are perfectly positively correlated, diversification does no good whatsoever. In reality, most stocks are positively correlated, but not perfectly so.

On average, the correlation coefficient for the returns on two randomly selected stocks would be close to +0.6, and for most pairs of stocks, ρ would lie in the range of +0.5 to +0.7. Under such conditions, combining stocks into a portfolio reduces risk but dos not eliminate it completely.

So in general, combining two stocks into a portfolio reduces the risk inherent in the individual stocks. What would happen if we included more than two stocks in the portfolio? As a rule, the risk of a portfolio will decline as the number of stock in the portfolio increases.

Before we move on to the next part, let's take a minute to show graphically the risk return combinations from varying the proportions of two risky assets and then to show how the graph of these combinations is affected by changes in the correlation coefficient for the returns on the two assets (Table 6-8, Table 6-9, Figure 6-1).

Table 6-8 Risk/Return Characteristics for Two Individual Assets

	A	B
Expected return (%)	11	25
Standard deviation (%)	15	20
Correlation	0.3	

Table 6-9 Possible Combinations of A and B

W_A (%)	100	80	60	40	20	0
W_B (%)	0	20	40	60	80	100
$E(R_p)$ (%)	11.0	13.8	16.6	19.4	22.2	25.0
σ_p (%)	15.0	13.7	13.7	14.9	17.1	20.0

The plot in Figure 6-1 represents all possible expected return and standard deviation combinations attainable by investing in varying amounts of A and B. We'll call it the risk-return trade-off curve.

If you have all your investment in A, your "portfolio" will have an expected return and standard deviation equal to that of A's and you will be at one end of the curve. As you increase your investment in B to 20 percent and decrease your investment in A to 80 percent, you will move up the risk-return trade-off curve to the point where the expected return is 13.8 percent with a standard deviation of 13.7 percent. Moving along the curve (and changing the expected return and standard deviation of the portfolio) is a matter of changing your portfolio allocation between the two stocks.

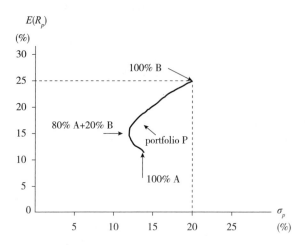

Figure 6-1   Risk-Return Trade-off Curve

We can create portfolios with the same risk level (i. e. , same standard deviation) and higher expected returns by diversifying our investment portfolio across many stocks. We can even benefit by adding just B to a portfolio of only A stock. We can create a combination of A and B (portfolio P) that has the same standard deviation but a higher expected return. Risk-averse investors would always prefer that combination to A by itself.

Let's take an analytical look at how diversification reduces risk by using the portfolio combinations in Figure 6-1. As indicated, the end points of this curve represent the risk-return combination from a 100 percent investment in either A or B. Notice that as B is added to A, the frontier "bulges" up and to the left. This bulge is what creates the diversification benefits because portfolios with between 60% and 80% allocations to A have both less risk and grater expected return than a portfolio of A only.

6.3.5   Special Role of Correlation

As the correlation between the two assets decreases, the benefits of diversification increase. That is because, as the correlation decreases, there is less of a tendency for stock returns to move together. The separate movements of each stock serve to reduce the volatility of the portfolio to a level that is less than that of its individual components.

Figure 6-2 illustrates the effects of correlation levels on diversification benefits. We have created the risk-return trade-off line for four different levels of correlation between the returns on two stocks.

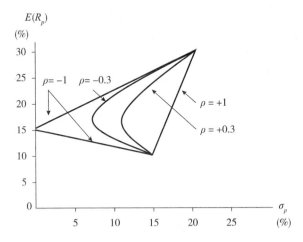

Figure 6-2   Effects of Correlation on Diversification Benefits

Notice that the amount of bulge in the risk-return trade-off line is a function of the correlation between the two assets: the lower the correlation (closer to -1), the greater the bulge; the larger the correlation (closer to +1), the smaller the bulge.

What does all this tell us? The lower the correlation, while all else equal, the greater the diversification benefits will be. This principle also applies to portfolios with many stocks.

The calculations required to generate what we called the risk-return trade-off curve for a two-asset portfolio are not too difficult to do with a spreadsheet. However, the statistical input requirements to apply Markowitz portfolio theory（马柯维茨资产组合理论）in a large portfolio are significant. Specifically, we must estimate:

The expected return for each asset available for investment;

The standard deviation for each asset;

The correlations between every pair of assets.

This need for correlations can be particularly onerous. For example, if the universe of potential securities includes 100 different stocks, then there are 4950 pair correlation coefficients that must be estimated.

However, with enough computer power, we can generate the set of efficient portfolios from all the possible combinations of all the assets available for investment. A portfolio is considered to be efficient if no other portfolio offers a higher expected return with the same risk or if no other portfolio offers lower risk with the same return. Efficient portfolio is a key concept in portfolio theory.

The efficient frontier represents the set of portfolios that will give you the highest return at each level of risk. Compare A with B, A has the same risk level with B (the same σ), while A has a higher rate of return than B, so investor has no reason to choose B. The efficient frontier is portrayed in Figure 6-3.

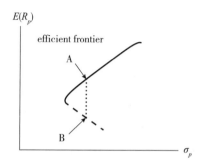

Figure 6-3   Markowitz Efficient Frontier (马柯维茨有效边界)

However, Markowitz's efficient frontier does not consider the existence of a risk-free asset. Adding a risk-free asset to theMarkowitz portfolio construction process allows portfolio theory to develop into capital market theory.

6.4   Capital Market Line

The introduction of a risk-free asset changes the Markowitz efficient frontier from a curve into a straight line called the capital market line (CML, 资本市场线).

Let's see how this conclusion is derived. If you invest a portion of your total funds in a risky portfolio X and the remaining portion in the risk-free asset, the equation for the expected return of the resulting portfolio will be:

$$E(R_p) = (1-w_X)r_f + w_X E(R_X) \tag{6-13}$$

$$= r_f + w_X[E(R_X) - r_f]$$

Where:

r_f = the risk-free rate

$E(R_X)$ = the expected return on portfolio X

w_X = percentage (weight) of the total portfolio value invested in portfolio X

$1-w_X$ = the percentage (weight) of the total portfolio value invested in the risk-free asset

If you combine the risk-free asset with a risky portfolio, the equation for the expected standard deviation of the resulting portfolio will be the same as a two-risky-asset portfolio:

$$\sigma_p = \sqrt{(1-w_X)^2\sigma_f^2 + w_X^2\sigma_X^2 + 2(1-w_X)w_X\sigma_f\sigma_X\rho_{f,X}} \tag{6-14}$$

Where:

σ_f = standard deviation of the risk-free asset

σ_X = standard deviation of the expected returns on portfolio X

$\rho_{f,X}$ = correlation between the risk-free asset and portfolio X

When one of the assets is risk-free, the calculation is much easier. By definition, under the assumptions of portfolio theory and capital market theory, if an asset is risk-free, its return does not vary. Thus, its variance and standard deviation are zero. If an asset has no variance, its expected return doesn't move. If the risk-free rate, r_f, is constant, it can't co-vary with other assets. In other words, the risk-free rate is stationary. Thus, its correlation coefficient with all other assets is zero.

Since $\sigma_f = 0$, $\rho_{f,X} = 0$, the equation for portfolio standard deviation is simplified to:

$$\sigma_p = w_X\sigma_X \tag{6-15}$$

If we put 40 percent of our portfolio assets in the risky portfolio, the resulting portfolio has 40 percent of the standard deviation of the risky portfolio. The risk-return relationship is now linear.

Combining this with our expected return equation (6-13), we get the following linear equation for the expected portfolio return as a function of portfolio standard deviation:

$$E(R_p) = r_f + \sigma_p \left\{ \frac{[E(R_X) - r_f]}{\sigma_X} \right\} \tag{6-16}$$

This line is called CML. It is the line representing combinations of the risk-free asset and a risky portfolio X and has an intercept of r_f and a slope equal to:

$$\frac{[E(R_X) - r_f]}{\sigma_X} \tag{6-17}$$

How do we select the optimal risky portfolio when a risk - free asset is also available? First, let's pick a risky portfolio that's on the Markowitz efficient frontier, since we know that these efficient portfolios dominate everything below them in terms of return offered for risk taken.

Now, let's combine the risk - free asset with portfolio X. Remember, the risk - return relationship resulting from the combination of the risk-free asset and a risky portfolio is a straight line.

Then, choose a risky portfolio that is above portfolio X on the efficient frontier, such as portfolio Y. Portfolios on the line from r_f to Y will be preferred to portfolios on the line from r_f to X because we get more return for a given amount of risk see Figure 6-4.

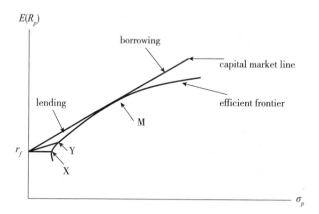

Figure 6-4   Capital Market Lines

Actually, we can keep getting better portfolios by moving up the efficient frontier. At point M you reach the best possible combination. Portfolio M is at the point where the risk-return trade-off line is just tangent to the efficient frontier. The line from r_f to M represents portfolios that are preferred among all the portfolios on the efficient frontier, except M.

Investors at point r_f have 100 percent of their funds invested in the risk-free asset. Investors at point M have 100 percent of their funds invested in portfolio M. Between r_f and M, investors hold both the risk-free asset and portfolio M. This means investors are lending some of their funds at the risk-free rate and investing the rest in portfolio M. To the right of M, investors hold more than 100 percent of portfolio M. This means they are borrowing funds to buy more of portfolio M.

What all investors have to do to get the risk and return combination that suits them is to simply vary the proportion of their investment in the risky portfolio M and the risk-free asset. So, in the CML world, all investors will hold some combination of the risk-free asset and portfolio M. Since all investors want to hold the same risky portfolio, risky portfolio M must be the market portfolio.

The market portfolio is the portfolio consisting of every risky asset; the weights on each asset are equal to the percentage of the market value of the asset to the market value of the entire market portfolio. For example, if the market value of a stock is $100 million and the market value of the market portfolio is $5 billion, that stock's weight in the market portfolio is 2 percent.

Logic tells us that the market portfolio, which will be held by all investors, has to contain all the stocks, bonds, and risky assets in existence because all assets have to be held by someone. This portfolio theoretically includes all risky assets, so it is completely diversified.

When you diversify across assets that are not perfectly correlated, the portfolio's risk is less than the weighted sum of the risks of the individual securities in the portfolio. The risk that disappears in the portfolio construction process is called the asset's unsystematic risk. Since the market portfolio contains all risky assets, it must represent the ultimate in diversification. All the risk that can be diversified away must be gone. The risk that is left cannot be diversified away, since there is nothing left to add to the portfolio. The risk that remains is called the systematic risk.

The concept of systematic risk applies to individual securities as well as to portfolios. Some securities are very sensitive to market changes. Typical examples of firms that are very sensitive to market movements are luxury goods manufacturers. These firms have high systematic risk. Other firms, such as utility companies, respond very little to changes in the overall market. These firms have very little systematic risk. Hence, total risk can be broken down into its component parts: unsystematic risk and systematic risk.

Do you actually have to buy all the securities in the market to diversify away unsystematic risk? No. Academic studies have shown that as you increase the number of stocks in a portfolio, the portfolio's risk falls toward the level of market risk. One study showed that it only took 30 securities. Whatever the number, it is significantly less than all the securities. Figure 6-5 provides a general representation of this concept. Note in the figure here that once you get to 30 or so securities in a portfolio, the standard deviation remains constant. The remaining risk is systematic, or non-diversifiable risk. We will develop this concept later when we discuss beta, a measure of systematic risk.

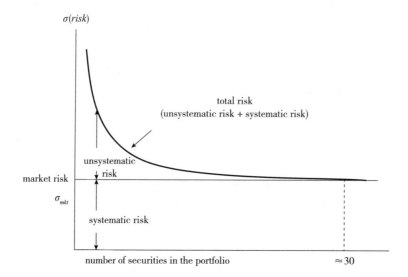

Figure 6-5   Risk vs. Number of Portfolio Assets

One important conclusion of capital markets theory is that equilibrium security returns depend on a stock's or a portfolio's systematic risk, not its total risk as measured by standard deviation. One of the assumptions of the model is that diversification is free. The reasoning is that investors will not be compensated for bearing risk that can be eliminated.

The implications of this conclusion are very important to asset pricing. The riskiest stock, with risk measured as standard deviation of returns, does not necessarily have the greatest expected return. Consider a biotech stock with one new drug product that is in clinical trials to determine its effectiveness. If it turns out that the drug is effective and safe, stock returns will be quite high. If, on the other hand, the subjects in the clinical trials are killed or otherwise harmed by the drug, the stock will fall to approximately zero and returns will be quite poor. This describes a stock with high standard deviation of returns.

The high risk of this biotech stock, however, is primarily from firm-specific factors so that its unsystematic risk is high. Since market factors such as economic growth rates have little to do with the eventual outcome for this stock, systematic risk is a small proportion of the total risk of the stock.

Capital market theory says that the equilibrium return on this stock may be less than that of a stock with much less firm-specific risk but more sensitivity to the factors that drive the return of the overall market. An established manufacturer of machine tools may not be a very risky investment in terms of total risk, but may have a greater sensitivity to market risk factors than biotech stock. Given this scenario, the stock with more total risk has less systematic risk and will therefore have a lower equilibrium rate of return according to capital markets theory.

Note that holding many biotech firms' stocks in a portfolio will diversify away the firm-specific risk. Some firms will have blockbuster products and some will fail, but you can imagine that when 50 or 100 such stocks are combined into a portfolio, the uncertainty about the portfolio return is much less than the uncertainty about the return of a single biotech firm's stock.

To sum up, unsystematic risk is not compensated in equilibrium because it can be eliminated for free through diversification. Systematic risk is measured by the contribution of a security to the risk of a well diversified portfolio and the expected equilibrium return on an individual security will depend on its systematic risk.

6.5　Security Market Line

Given that the only relevant risk for an individual asset i is the covariance between the asset's returns and the return on the market, $\text{Cov}_{i,mkt}$, we can plot the relationship between risk and return for individual assets using $\text{Cov}_{i,mkt}$ as our measure of systematic risk. The resulting line, plotted in Figure 6-6 is one version of what is referred to as the security market line (SML, 证券市场线).

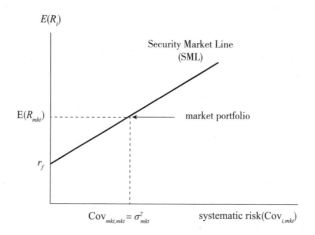

Figure 6-6 Security Market Line

The linear equation of the SML is:

$$E(R_i) = r_f + \frac{E(R_{mkt}) - r_f}{\sigma^2_{mkt}}(\text{Cov}_{i,mkt}) \qquad (6-18)$$

Which can be rearranged and stated as:

$$E(R_i) = r_f + \frac{\text{Cov}_{i,mkt}}{\sigma^2_{mkt}}[E(R_{mkt}) - r_f] \qquad (6-19)$$

The line described by the last equation is presented in Figure 6-7, where we let the standardized covariance term, $\dfrac{\text{Cov}_{i,mkt}}{\sigma^2_{mkt}}$, be defined as beta, β_i. This is the most common means of describing the SML, and the equation for this line is known as the capital asset pricing model (CAPM).

So we can define beta, $\beta_i = \dfrac{\text{Cov}_{i,mkt}}{\sigma^2_{mkt}}$, as a standardized measure of systematic risk.

Beta measures the sensitivity of a security's returns to changes in the market return.

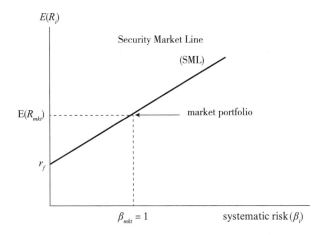

Figure 6-7　The Capital Asset Pricing Model (资本资产定价模型)

As we mentioned, when the SML is expressed in terms of beta, it is called the capital asset pricing model (CAPM). CAPM is stated as:

$$E(R_i) = r_f + \beta_i [E(R_{mkt}) - r_f] \tag{6-20}$$

The CAPM holds that, in equilibrium, the expected return on risky asset $E(R_i)$ is the risk-free rate, r_f, plus a beta-adjusted market risk premium, $\beta_i [E(R_{mkt}) - r_f]$.

It is important that you recognize that the CML and SML are very different. Recall the equation of the CML:

$$E(R_p) = r_f + \sigma_p \left\{ \frac{[E(R_X) - r_f]}{\sigma_X} \right\}$$

The CML uses total risk $= \sigma_p$ on the X-axis. Hence, only efficient portfolios will plot on the CML. On the other hand, the SML uses beta (systematic risk) on the X-axis, so in a CAPM world, all properly priced securities and portfolios of securities will plot on the SML.

The CAPM is one of the most fundamental concepts in investment theory. The CAPM is an equilibrium model that predicts the expected return on a stock, given the expected return on the market, the stock's beta coefficient, and the risk-free rate.

Example: The expected return on the market is 15 percent, the risk-free rate is 8 percent, and the beta for stock A (β_A) is 1.2. Compute the rate of return that would be expected (required) on this stock.

Answer:

$$E(R_A) = 0.08 + 1.2(0.15 - 0.08) = 0.164$$

In a CAPM world, all asset returns should fall on the SML. The SML tells us an asset's required return given its level of systematic risk (as measured by beta). The way we can use this CAPM theory to identify mis-priced securities is to compare an asset's estimated return to the required return according to the SML. If the returns are not equal, the asset is either overvalued or undervalued and an appropriate trading strategy may be implemented allordingly.

An asset with an expected return greater than its required return from the SML is undervalued; we should buy it.

An asset with an expected return less than its required return from the SML is overvalued; we should sell it.

As asset with an expected return equal to its required return from the SML is properly valued; we're indifferent between buying or selling it.

Example: Table 6−10 contains information based on analyst's forecasts for three stocks. Assume a risk−free rate of 7 percent and a market return of 15 percent. Compute the expected and required return on each stock, determine whether each stock is undervalued, overvalued, or properly valued, and outline an appropriate trading strategy.

Table 6−10   Forecast Data

Stock	Price today	E(price) in 1 year	E(dividend) in 1 year	Beta
A	$25	$27	$1.00	1.0
B	$40	$45	$2.00	0.8
C	$15	$17	$0.50	1.2

Answer: Expected and required returns computations are shown in Table 6−11.

Table 6-11 Forecast Returns vs. Required Returns

	Forecast return (%)	Required return (%)
A	($ 27- $ 25+ $ 1)/ $ 25 = 12. 0	0. 07+(1. 0)(0. 15-0. 07) = 15. 0
B	($ 45- $ 40+ $ 2)/ $ 40 = 17. 5	0. 07+(0. 8)(0. 15-0. 07) = 13. 4
C	($ 17- $ 15+ $ 0. 5)/ $ 15 ≈ 16. 6	0. 07+(1. 2)(0. 15-0. 07) = 16. 6

Stock A is overvalued. It is expected to earn 12 percent, but based on its systematic risk it should earn 15 percent. It plots below the SML.

Stock B is undervalued. It is expected to earn 17. 5 percent, but based on its systematic risk it should earn 13. 4 percent. It plots above the SML.

Stock C is properly valued. It is expected to earn 16. 6 percent, and based on its systematic risk it should earn 16. 6 percent. It plots on the SML.

The appropriate trading strategy is:

Sell stock A, buy stock B, and buy/sell/ignore stock C.

Experiment 5
Excel Implementation for Beta

用 Excel 解决 BETA 系数问题

例：A 公司（Firm A）连续 15 个月的月末收盘价及所在市场的综合指数收盘点数如表 6-12 所示，则 Firm A 的 beta 系数是多少（见表 6-12）？

表 6-12　求解 beta 系数

	A	B	C	D	E	F	G	H	I	J	K
1											
2		Firm A's beta		−0.6145	→→→		=COVAR(D7:D20,J7:J20)/VARP(D7:D20)				
3											
4			Index					Firm A			
5		Month	Closing price	Monthly return	=LN(C7/C6)		Month	Closing Price	Monthly return	=LN(I7/I6)	
6		1	3318.19				1	4.876			
7		2	3188.72	−3.98%			2	5.112	4.73%		
8		3	3009.88	−5.77%			3	5.343	4.42%		
9		4	2876.14	−4.55%			4	5.227	−2.19%		
10		5	2800.47	−2.67%			5	6.091	15.30%		
11		6	2900.56	3.51%			6	7.122	15.64%		
12		7	2918.31	0.61%			7	6.895	−3.24%		
13		8	3000.45	2.78%			8	7.327	6.08%		
14		9	3288.76	9.17%			9	7.001	−4.55%		
15		10	3455.21	4.94%			10	6.775	−3.28%		
16		11	3600.89	4.13%			11	6.343	−6.59%		
17		12	3900.32	7.99%			12	6.002	−5.53%		
18		13	3877.56	−0.59%			13	6.123	2.00%		
19		14	3891.34	0.35%			14	6.554	6.80%		
20		15	4001.24	2.79%			15	6.881	4.87%		

Experiment 6
Excel Implementation for Portfolio

用 Excel 解决资产组合风险收益问题

例：股票 A 和股票 B 连续 13 个月的月末收盘价如表 6-13 所示，根据此表，求解以下问题。

（1）两支股票各自的月均收益率、收益率方差、收益率标准差是多少？

（2）两支股票的相关系数是多少？

（3）若股票 A 和股票 B 构建投资组合，股票 A 的投资权重为 40%，则该组合的预期收益率及收益率标准差、收益率方差是多少？

（4）由股票 A 和股票 B 构建投资组合，将所有可能的收益风险绘图。

表 6-13 求解资产组合风险收益

	A	B	C	D	E	F	G	H	I	J	K	L	M	N
1					资产组合风险收益									
2		Stock A						Stock B						
3	month	price	return	return-mean			month	price	return	return-mean		product		
4	0	25.00			=LN(B5/B4)		0	45.00					=D5*J5	
5	1	24.12	-3.58%	-6.82%			1	44.85	-0.33%	-3.80%		0.00259		
6	2	23.37	-3.16%	-6.40%	=C5-$C$18		2	46.88	4.43%	0.96%		-0.00061		
7	3	24.75	5.74%	2.50%			3	45.25	-3.54%	-7.01%		-0.00175		
8	4	26.62	7.28%	4.04%			4	50.87	11.71%	8.24%		0.00333		
9	5	26.50	-0.45%	-3.69%			5	53.25	4.57%	1.10%		-0.00041		
10	6	28.00	5.51%	2.27%			6	53.25	0.00%	-3.47%		-0.00079		
11	7	28.88	3.09%	-0.15%			7	62.75	16.42%	12.95%		-0.00019		
12	8	29.75	2.97%	-0.27%			8	65.50	4.29%	0.82%		-0.00002		
13	9	31.38	5.33%	2.09%			9	66.87	2.07%	-1.40%		-0.00029		
14	10	36.25	14.43%	11.19%			10	78.50	16.03%	12.57%		0.01406		
15	11	37.13	2.40%	-0.84%			11	78.00	-0.64%	-4.11%		0.00035		
16	12	36.88	-0.68%	-3.92%			12	68.23	-13.38%	-16.85%		0.00660		
17														
18	monthly mean		3.24%		=AVERAGE(C5:C16)		monthly mean		3.47%					
19	monthly variance		0.23%		=VARP(C5:C16)		monthly variance		0.65%					
20	monthly stand.dev		4.78%				monthly stand.dev		8.03%					
21					=STDEVP(C5:C16)									

Continued

	A	B	C	D	E	F	G	H	I
22			=AVERAGE(L5:L16)				=C24/(C20*120)		
23	portfolio cov		0.00191	correlatioin	0.49589				
24			0.00191		0.49589	=CORREL(C5:C16,I5:I16)			
25	proportion		0.4				proportion	sigma	mean
26	month	r(A)	r(B)	r(p)				sigma	mean
27	1	-3.58%	-0.33%	-1.63%	=B27*$C$25+C27*(1-$C$25)		0	8.03%	3.47%
28	2	-3.16%	4.43%	1.39%			0.2	6.95%	3.42%
29	3	5.74%	-3.54%	0.17%			0.3	6.46%	3.40%
30	4	7.28%	11.71%	9.94%			0.4	6%	3.38%
31	5	-0.45%	4.57%	2.56%			0.5	5.60%	3.35%
32	6	5.51%	0.00%	2.20%			0.6	5.26%	3.33%
33	7	3.09%	16.42%	11.09%			0.7	5%	3.31%
34	8	2.97%	4.29%	3.76%			0.8	4.83	3.29%
35	9	5.33%	2.07%	3.38%			0.9	4.75	3.26%
36	10	14.43%	16.03%	15.39%			1	4.78%	3.24%
37	11	2.40%	-0.64%	0.58%					
38	12	-0.68%	-13.38%	-8.30%					
39									
40	mean	3.38%	=AVERAGE(D27:D38)						
41	variance	0.36%	=VARP(D27:D38)						
42	st. dev	6.00%	=STDEVP(D27:D38)						
43									
44			=STDEVP(D27:D38)						
45									

=COVAR(C5:C16,I5:I16)

资产组合风险收益

本章小结

一、本章要点与难点

（1）单个风险资产。

$$收益: E(R) = \sum_{i=1}^{n} P_i R_i, \quad E(R) = \overline{R} = \frac{\sum_{t=1}^{n} R_t}{n}$$

$$风险: \sigma^2 = \sum_{i=1}^{n} P_i \left[R_i - E(R) \right]^2$$

$$\sigma = \sqrt{\sigma^2}$$

$$CV = \frac{\sigma}{\hat{r}}$$

$$\beta = \frac{Cov_{i,mkt}}{\sigma_{mkt}^2}$$

（2）资产组合。

$$收益: E(R_p) = \sum_{i=1}^{n} w_i E(R_i)$$

风险: $Cov_{1,2} = \sum\limits_{i=1}^{n} \{P_i [R_{i,1} - E(R_1)] [R_{i,2} - E(R_2)]\}$

$$\rho_{1,2} = \frac{Cov_{1,2}}{\sigma_1 \sigma_2}$$

$$\sigma_p = \sqrt{\sigma_p^2} = \sqrt{\sum\limits_{i}^{n} w_i^2 \sigma_i^2 + \sum\limits_{i=1}^{n} \sum\limits_{j=1}^{n} w_i w_j Cov_{i,j}} \ (i \neq j)$$

(3) 明确 CML 和 SML 的区别。

二、Self-Test Problems

6-1　An analyst has been given information (see Table 6-14) on three portfolios. (Assume that only these three portfolios exist. Also, assume that the risk free rate is 6 percent)

Table 6-14　Information

	A	B	C
Expected return (%)	14	9	16
Expected risk (%)	12	10	14

Using the information provided above, the analyst should combine which portfolio with the risk free asset?

6-2　Tim Woods wants to calculate the required return for APC to help him determine whether or not to recommend the stock. The latest consensus was an expected return of 3. 0 percent. The risk free rate is 4. 0 percent and the market risk premium is 3. 5 percent. The covariance of APC and the market is−0. 050. The standard deviations of APC and the market are 0. 35 and 0. 25, respectively. What should Woods calculate as the stock's beta, and should he recommend a buy or sell of the stock (considering the investment on a stand alone basis)?

	Beta	Recommendation
A.	−0. 2	Buy
B.	−0. 8	Sell
C.	−0. 8	Buy
D.	+0. 8	Sell

6-3　Which of the following statements about the capital market line (CML) and security market line (SML) is FALSE?

    A. The slope of the SML is the market risk premium.

    B. Any security on the CML is properly priced.

    C. The CML is formed by adding the risk free asset to the efficient frontier.

    D. The CML graphs systematic risk only.

  6-4 A stock's expected return has the following distribution (Table 6-15):

Table 6-15 Distribution of ROR

Demand for the Company's Products	Probability of this Demand Occurring	Rate of return if this Demand Occurs
Weak	0.1	-50%
Below average	0.2	-5%
Average	0.4	16%
Above average	0.2	25%
Strong	0.1	60%

Calculate the stock's expected return, standard deviation, and coefficient of variation.

  6-5 Stock A and Stock B have following expected return and distribution (Table 6-16):

Table 6-16 Expected Return and Distribution

Probability	Expected return (%)	
	A	B
0.1	6.0	14.0
0.2	8.0	12.0
0.3	10.0	10.0
0.4	12.0	8.0
0.1	14.0	6.0

Calculate the covariance and correlation between Stock A and Stock B.

  6-6 A portfolios consists of 50% Stock A and 50% Stock B, and the expected return are 12% and 8% respectively, standard deviation are both 9%. What is the standard deviation under different correlation (ρ_{AB} = +1, +0.5, 0.0, -0.5, -1.0)?

Chapter 7
Capital Budgeting
（资本预算）

This chapter provides an overview of the firm's capital budgetary system—The process of evaluating specific investment decisions. Here the term 'capital' refers to operating assets used in production, while a budgeting is the whole process of analyzing projects and deciding which ones to include in the capital budget.

Capital budgeting is perhaps the most important task faced by financial managers and their staffs. You need to know how to calculate all of the measures used to evaluate capital projects and the decision rules associated with them.

Capital projects may be classified as follows:

Mutually exclusive projects mean that only one project in a set of possible projects can be accepted.

Independent projects are projects that are unrelated to each other. If you have unlimited funds, you may accept or reject any combination of independent projects.

In deciding whether to accept a new project, we will focus on cash flows. Cash flows represent the benefits generated from accepting a capital-budgeting proposal.

7.1　Decision Method（决策方法）

Now we will look at the process of decision making with respect to investment in fixed assets. That is, should a proposed project be accepted or should it be rejected. Each of these methods below is used frequently in the real world.

7. 1. 1　Payback Period Method（投资回收期）

The payback period（PBP）is the number of years it takes to recover the initial cost of an investment.

The accept/reject criterion involves whether the project's payback period is less than or equal to the firm's maximum desired payback period. The shorter the payback period, the better the project.

As this criterion measures how quickly the projectwill return its original investment, it deals with cash flows rather than accounting profits. It also ignores the time value of money and cash flows beyond the payback period. This means terminal or salvage value wouldn't be considered.

Example：Calculate the payback periods for the two projects that have the cash flows presented in Table 7−1. Note the year 0 cash flow represents the net cost of each of the projects.

Table 7−1　Expected Net After−Tax Cash Flows

Year（t）	Project A（$）	Project B（$）
0	−2000	−2000
1	1000	200
2	800	600
3	600	800
4	200	1200

Answer：Note that the cumulative net cash flow（NCF）is just the running total of the cash flows at the end of each time period. Payback will occur when the cumulative NCF equals zero. To find the payback periods, construct a table like Table 7−2.

Table 7-2 Cumulative Net Cash Flows

	Year (t)	0	1	2	3	4
Project A	Net cash flow	−2000	1000	800	600	200
	Cumulative NCF	−2000	−1000	−200	400	600
Project B	Net cash flow	−2000	200	600	800	1200
	Cumulative NCF	−2000	−1800	−1200	−400	800

The payback period is determined from the cumulative net cash flow table as follows:

Payback period = Years until full recovery +

$$\frac{\text{unrecovered cost at the beginning of the last year}}{\text{cash flow during the last year}}$$

$$\text{Payback period A} = 2 + \frac{200}{600}^① = 2.33 \text{ years}$$

$$\text{Payback period B} = 3 + \frac{400}{1200} = 3.33 \text{ years}$$

Generally speaking, the shorter a project's payback, the better the project. To decide which project to accept, the firm must first establish a benchmark payback period.

Decision rule: payback ≤ the benchmark payback, accept the project;

payback > the benchmark payback, reject the project.

As for this example, presume that the firm requires a payback period of three and a half years if A and B are independent, accept project A and B; if A and B are mutually exclusive, then project A would be accepted rather than B.

7.1.2 Discounted Payback Period (贴现的投资回收期)

The discounted payback period is defined as the number of years required to recover the investment from discounted net cash flows, or say it is the number of years it takes for a project to return its initial investment in current (present value) dollars.

---

① After two years, the project has collect $1800 together, still left $200 to be collected. While the third year will earn $600, so we only need 200/600 = 1/3 of the third year to recover the total investment.

An important drawback of both the payback and discounted payback methods is that they ignore cash flows that are paid or received after the payback period. Although the payback methods have serious faults, they do provide information on how long funds will be tied up in a project. So both the payback and discounted payback give us an indication of a project's risk and liquidity, since distant cash flows are riskier than near cash flows.

Example: Compute the discounted payback period for projects A and B described in Table 7-3. Assume that the firm's cost of capital is 10 percent.

Table 7-3 Cash Flows for Project A and B

	Year (t)	0	1	2	3	4
	Net cash flow	-2000	1000	800	600	200
Project A	Discounted NCF	-2000	910	661	451	137
	Cumulative NCF	-2000	-1090	-429	22	159
	Net cash flow	-2000	200	600	800	1200
Project B	Discounted NCF	-2000	182	496	601	820
	Cumulative NCF	-2000	-1818	-1322	-721	99

Answer:

$$\text{Discounted payback period A} = 2 + \frac{429}{451} = 2.95 \text{ years}$$

$$\text{Discounted payback period B} = 3 + \frac{721}{820} = 3.88 \text{ years}$$

Decision rule: payback ≤ the benchmark payback, accept the project;

payback > the benchmark payback, reject the project.

As for this example, assume the firm's maximum discounted payback period is four years. If A and B are independent, accept project A and B. If A and B are mutually exclusive, then project A would be accepted rather than B.

7.1.3 Net Present Value (NPV, 净现值)

The net present value (NPV) method is the amount of cash flow (in present value terms by cost of capital) that the project generated after repaying the invested capital (project cost). To implement this approach, we proceed as follows:

①Find the present value of each cash flow, including all inflows and outflows, discounted at the project's cost of capital.

②Sum these discounted cash flows; this sum is defined as the project's NPV.

The equation for the NPV is as follows:

$$NPV = CF_0 + \frac{CF_1}{(1+r)^1} + \frac{CF_2}{(1+r)^2} + \cdots + \frac{CF_n}{(1+r)^n}$$

$$= \sum_{t=0}^{n} \frac{CF_t}{(1+r)^t} \qquad (7-1)$$

Here CF_t is the expected net cash flow at period t, r is the project's cost of capital, and n is its life. Cash outflows are treated as negative cash flows.

A positive NPV project increases shareholders' wealth, and a negative NPV project decreases shareholders' wealth. For independent projects, the NPV decision rule is to accept the project if NPV > 0. For mutually exclusive projects, choose the one with higher NPV, as long as its NPV is greater than 0.

Example: Using the projects described in Table 7-1, compute the NPV of each project's cash flows and determine which project should be accepted if:

①the projects are independent, ②the projects are mutually exclusive.

Answer:

$$NPV_A = -2000 + \frac{1000}{1.1^1} + \frac{800}{1.1^2} + \frac{600}{1.1^3} + \frac{200}{1.1^4} = 157.64$$

$$NPV_B = -2000 + \frac{200}{1.1^1} + \frac{600}{1.1^2} + \frac{800}{1.1^3} + \frac{1200}{1.1^4} = 98.35$$

Decision rule: If project A and B are independent, accept both. If project A and B are mutually exclusive, A has the higher NPV and would, therefore, be accepted.

7.1.4 Internal Rate of Return (IRR, 内部收益率)

The IRR is defined as the rate of return on which the net present value of a project is zero.

$$NPV = 0 = CF_0 + \frac{CF_1}{(1+IRR)^1} + \frac{CF_2}{(1+IRR)^2} + \cdots + \frac{CF_n}{(1+IRR)^n} = \sum_{t=0}^{n} \frac{CF_t}{(1+IRR)^t}$$

$$(7-2)$$

To calculate the IRR you may use the trial-and error method. That is guessing IRRs until you get the right one. For a realistic project with a fairly long life, the trial-and error approach is a tedious, time-consuming task. Fortunately, it is easy to find IRR with a financial calculator. It is also easy to find the IRR using the spreadsheet in Excel.

IRR decision rule: First, define the minimumrate the firm will accept a given project. This is usually the firm's cost of capital.

Then, for independent projects: IRR $\geqslant$ the cost of capital, accept the project; IRR< the cost of capital, reject the project.

For mutually exclusive projects, choose all projects with IRR $\geqslant$ cost of capital.

7.1.5　Rationale for the IRR Method

The IRR is based on this logic: ①The IRR on a project is its expected rate of return. ②If the internal rate of return exceeds the cost of the funds used to finance the project, a surplus will remain after paying the capital cost, and this surplus will accrue to the firm's stockholders. On the other hand, if the internal rate of return is less than the cost of capital, then taking on the project will impose a cost on current stockholders.

Example: Continuing with the cash flows presented in Table 7-1 for project A and B, compute the IRR for each project and recommend acceptance under the assumptions: ①The projects are independent, ②They are mutually exclusive.

Answer:

Project A:

$$NPV = 0 = -2000 + \frac{1000}{(1+IRR_A)^1} + \frac{800}{(1+IRR_A)^2} + \frac{600}{(1+IRR_A)^3} + \frac{200}{(1+IRR_A)^4}$$

Project B:

$$NPV = 0 = -2000 + \frac{200}{(1+IRR_B)^1} + \frac{600}{(1+IRR_B)^2} + \frac{800}{(1+IRR_B)^3} +$$

$$\frac{1200}{(1+IRR_B)^4}$$

For project A, when we try $IRR = 15\%$, we get $NPV = -16.66$; then we

try $IRR = 14\%$, we get $NPV = 16.17$, so $IRR = 14\% + \dfrac{16.17}{16.17 - (-16.66)}$

$(15\% - 14\%) = 14.5\%$.

And use the same trial-and-error method, we get IRR on project B is 11.8%.

The NPV method implicitly assumes that the rate at which cash flows can be rein-vested is the cost of capital, whereas the IRR method assumes that the firm can reinvest at the IRR. Which is the better assumption—that cash flows can be reinvested at the cost of capital, or that they can be reinvested at the project's IRR? The best assumption is that projects' cash flows can be reinvested at the cost of capital, which means that the NPV method is more reliable.

Note that, when projects are independent, the NPV and IRR methods both lead to exactly the same accept or reject decision. However, when evaluating mutually exclusive projects, especially those that differ in scale and/or timing, the NPV method should be used.

7.1.6 The NPV Profile

A project's NPV profile is a graph that plots the project's NPV at different discount rates. Remember, when you change the discount rate, you also change the NPV. The discount rates are located along the x-axis of the NPV profile, and the corresponding NPVs are plotted on the y-axis.

Note that the projects' IRR are located where the NPV profiles intersect the x-axis when the NPV is zero. This is because, by definition, the IRR is the discount rate that makes the NPV zero.

Using the projects described in Table 7-1, with different capital cost, we can get different NPV. We set few of them in the Table 7-4.

Table 7-4   Pairs of Different Discount Rate and Its NPV

Discount rate	NPV_A	NPV_B
0%	600.00	800.00
5%	360.84	413.00
10%	157.64	98.36
15%	(16.66)	(160.28)

Now, let's draw the NPV profile for both A and B (see Figure 7-1).

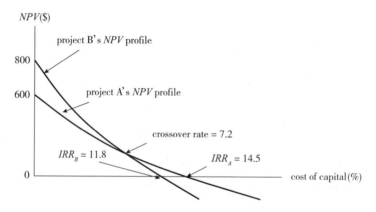

Figure 7-1   NPV Profile of Project A and B

Also notice that the NPV profiles intersect at the discount rate that makes the NPV of both projects equal.

7.1.7   Modified Internal Rate of Return (MIRR, 修正内部收益率)

In spite of a strong academic preference for NPV, managers find it intuitively more appealing to evaluate investments in terms of percentage rates of return than dollars of NPV. So we can modify the IRR and make it a better indicator of relative profitability. The new measure is called the modified IRR or MIRR, and it is defined as follows:

$$\sum_{t=0}^{n} \frac{COF_t}{(1+r)^t} = \frac{\sum\limits_{t=0}^{n} CIF_t (1+r)^{n-t}}{(1+MIRR)^n} \tag{7-3}$$

$$PV \text{ of Costs} = \frac{terminal\ value}{(1+MIRR)^n}$$

Here COF refers to cash outflows (negative numbers) , or the cost of the project, and CIF refers to cash inflows (positive numbers) , r is the cost of capital.

We can illustrate the calculation with Project's MIRR in Figure 7-2:

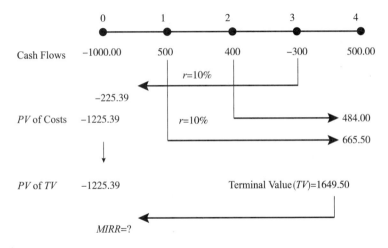

Figure 7-2   The Calculation with Project's MIRR

$$PV \text{ of Costs} = \frac{Terminal\ Value}{(1+MIRR)^n}$$

$$1225.39 = \frac{1649.50}{(1+MIRR)^4}$$

$$MIRR = 7.71\%$$

The modified IRR has a significant advantage over the regular IRR. MIRR assumes that cash flows from all projects are reinvested at the cost of capital, while the regular IRR assumes that the cash flows from each project are reinvested at the project's own IRR.

Our conclusion is that the MIRR is superior to the regular IRR as an indicator of a project's true rate of return, or expected long-term rate of return, but the NPV method is still the best way to choose among competing projects because it provides the best indication of how much each project will add to the value of the firm.

7.1.8 Project with Unequal Lives

When choosing between two mutually exclusive alternatives with significantly different lives, an adjustment is necessary. We now discuss two methods: The replacement chain (common life) method and the equivalent annual annuity (EAA) method.

Example: Somy Inc. has two alternative projects. ①Project A has a useful life of 6 years. ②Project B has a useful life of 3 years. The time lines presented in Figure 7-3 and Figure 7-4 show the cash flows, NPVs, and IRRs for both of these (mutually exclusive) projects.

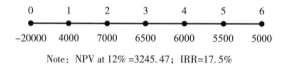

Note: NPV at 12% =3245.47; IRR=17.5%

Figure 7-3　Expected Cash Flows for A

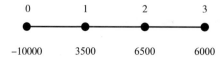

Note: NPV at 12% =2577.44; IRR=25.20%

Figure 7-4　Expected Cash Flows for B

Evaluate these projects using both the replacement chain and equivalent annual annuity approaches.

Answer:

(1) Replacement chain (common life, 最小公倍法) method.

To make the comparison meaningful, we can find the NPV for the two projects over a common life.

In this case, the common life is 6 years. This means that, for project B, we will need to restart another 3-year project in year 3 to make it comparable to the 6-year project A. Assuming no changes in annual cash flows and a constant cost of capital of 12 percent, we can compute the NPV of the two projects using the process illustrated in Figure 7-5.

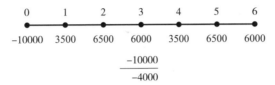

Note: NPV at 12%=4412.01; IRR=25.2%

Figure 7-5   Replacement Chain for Offset Printer

Decision: The NPV of this extended project B is 4412, and its IRR is 25.2%. Since the extended NPV (4412.01) of two chained-together 3-year project B (six years total) is greater than the NPV (3245.47) of the project A, project B should be selected.

Figure 7-6 illustrates that the value of the cash flow streams of two projects can be summarized by their NPV: One at year 0 representing the value of the initial project, and one at year 3representing the value of the replication project.

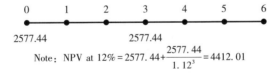

Note: NPV at 12% = $2577.44 + \dfrac{2577.44}{1.12^3} = 4412.01$

Figure 7-6   Replacement Chain NPV

(2) Equivalent annual annuity (EAA, 年均净现值法) approach.

The EAA approach is a simpler approach to evaluate mutually exclusive projects with different lives. What we should do is to convert the NPV of each alternative to an annual amount. There are threesteps in the EAA approach.

Step 1：find each project's NPV.

$$NPV_A \approx 3245$$
$$NPV_B \approx 2577$$

Step 2：find an annuity (EAA) that equates to the project's NPV over its individual life at the WACC.

EAA_A ： PV = -3245; FV = 0; N = 6; I = 12%; compute PMT = 789

EAA_B ： PV = -2577; FV = 0; N = 3; I = 12%; compute PMT = 1073

Step 3：select the project with the highest EAA. In this example project B should be accepted because $EAA_B > EAA_A$.

7.1.9 Capital Rationing (资本限量决策)

Ideally, firms will continue to invest in positive NPV projects until their marginal returns equal their marginal cost of capital. Should a firm have insufficient capital to do this, it must ration its capital (allocate its funds) among the best possible combination of acceptable projects. So, capital rationing may be defined as the allocation of a fixed amount of capital among a set of available projects that will maximize shareholders' wealth. A firm with less capital than profitable projects' need should choose the combination of projects that they can afford to fund and has the greatest total NPV.

7.2 Cash Flow Estimation (现金流测算)

The basic principles of capital budgeting have been covered, given a project's expected cash flows, it is easy to calculate its payback, discounted payback, NPV, IRR and MIRR. Unfortunately, cash flows are rarely given. Rather, managers must estimate them based on information collected from sources both inside and outside the company.

The most important, but also the most difficult work in capital budgeting is estimating projects' cash flows.

Analysts often make errors in estimating cash flows, but two cardinal rules can help you minimize mistakes：①Capital budgeting decisions must be based on cash flows, not accounting income. ②Only incremental cash flows are relevant.

7.2.1　Cash Flows vs. Accounting Income

In capital budgeting, we use annual net cash flows (NCF) or free cash flow (FCF), not accounting income, to make our decision. We can define net cash flow as：

$$\text{Net cash flow (NCF)} = \text{net income+depreciation}$$

Net cash flows should reflect all non−cash charges, not just depreciation. Depreciation is usually the largest non−cash charge for a firm.

$$\text{Free cash flow (FCF)} = \text{net operating profit after taxes (NOPAT)}[1] + $$
$$\text{depreciation}[2]\text{−gross fixed asset expenditures}[3]−$$
$$\text{change in net working capital (}\Delta\text{NWC)}[4]$$

7.2.2　Incremental Cash Flows (增量现金流量)

Incremental cash flows are cash flows that occur if, and only if, the project is accepted. These cash flows represent the change in the total cash flow for the firm as a result of the acceptance of a project.

---

[1]　Net Operating Profit After Taxes (NOPAT) = EBIT(1−T).

[2]　In calculating net income, accountants usually subtract depreciation from revenues, but depreciation itself is not a cash flow. Therefore, depreciation must be added back to net income when estimating a project's cash flow.

[3]　Most projects require assets, and asset purchases represent negative cash flows. Even though the acquisition of assets results in a cash outflow, accountants do not show the purchase of fixed assets as a deduction from accounting income. Instead, they deduct a depreciation expense each year throughout the life of the asset. (Note that the full cost of fixed assets includes any shipping and installation costs)

[4]　Change in net operating working capital = Δoperating current assets−Δoperating current liabilities.

Normally, additional inventories are required to supporta new operation, and expanded sales tie up additional funds in accounts receivable. The difference between the required increase in operating current assets and the increase in operating current liabilities is the change in net operating working capital.

If this change is positive, as it generally is for expansion projects, then additional financing, over and above the cost of the fixed assets, will be needed. If it is negative, the project will free up cash and create a cash inflow.

Note that at the termination of the project, the firm will receive an end−of−project cash inflow (or outflow) when the need for the additional working capital ends.

Some issues that must be addressed when determining incremental cash flows are:

Sunk cost (沉没成本): A sunk cost is an outlay that has already occurred. Since sunk costs are not incremental costs, they should not be included in the analysis. An example of sunk costs is a consulting fee paid to a marketing research firm to estimate demand for a new product.

Opportunity cost (机会成本): Opportunity cost are cash flows that a firm is passing up by acquiring the asset in question. In other words, these are cash flows that would have been provided from an asset the firm already owns, had that asset not been used for the project under consideration.

Externalities (附加效应): Externalities refer to the effects the acceptance of a project may have on other parts of the firm. The primary externality is referred to as cannibalization, which occurs when a new project takes sales from an existing product. When considering externalities, the full implication of the new project (loss in sales of existing products) should be taken into account.

Generally, we can classify cash flows as ①initial investment outlay, ②operating cash flow over a project's life, ③terminal-year cash flow.

(1) Initial outlay (初始现金流量).

The initial outlay involves the immediate cash outflow necessary to purchase the asset and put it in operating order. This amount includes the cost of installing the asset and any non-expense cash outlays, such as increased working-capital requirements. Finally, if the investment decision is a replacement decision, the cash inflow associated with the selling price of the old asset, in addition to any tax effects resulting from its sale, must be included.

Potentially one of the most confusing initial outlay calculations is for a replacement project involving the incremental tax payment associated with the sale of an old asset. There are three possible tax situations dealing with the sale of an old asset:

1) The old asset is sold for a price above the depreciated value. Here the difference between the old asset's selling price and its depreciated value is considered a taxable gain and taxed at the marginal corporate tax rate.

2) The old asset is sold for its depreciated value. In this case, there is no tax result, as there is neither a gain nor a loss in the asset's sale.

3) The old asset is sold for less than its depreciated value. In this case the differ-

ence between the depreciated book value and the salvage value of the asset is a taxable loss and may be used to offset ordinary income and thus results in tax savings.

Example: Consider a company in the 40 percent marginal tax rate. This company is considering the purchase of a new machine for $ 50000 to be used in manufacturing. It has a five-year life and will be depreciated using the simplified straight line method.

The new machine will replace an existing machine, originally purchased for $ 30000 ten years ago, which currently has five more years of expected useful life. The existing machine will generate $ 2000 of depreciation expenses for each of the next five years, at which time the book value will be equal to zero.

To put the new machine in running order, it is necessary to pay after-tax shipping charges of $ 2000 and installation charges of $ 3000. Because the new machine will work faster than the old one, it will require an increase in goods-in-process inventory of $ 5000.

Finally, the old machine can be sold for $ 15000.

The net initial outlay associated with this project is $ 47000. These calculations are summarized in Table 7-5.

Table 7-5　Calculation of Initial Outlay for Example Problem ($)

Outflows:		
Purchase price	-50000	
Shipping fee	-2000	
Installation fee	-3000	
Installed cost of machine		-55000
Increased taxes from sale of old machine		
($ 15000- $ 10000) ×0. 40		-2000
Increased investment in inventory		-5000[1]
Total outflows		-62000

[1]　In effect, the firm invests $ 5000 in inventory now, resulting in an initial cash outlay, and liquidates this inventory in five years, resulting in a cash inflow at the end of the project.

	Continued
Inflows:	
Salvage value of old machine	+15000[①]
Net initial outlay	−47000

（2）Operating Cash Flows（经营现金流量）.

Operating cash flows are the incremental cash inflows over the capital asset's economic life.

Operating cash flows are defined as:

Operation Cash flow $=[$ (revenue$-$cost$-$depreciation)(1$-t$)$]+$depreciation[②]

$\qquad = $ (revenue$-$cost)(1$-t$)$+$depreciation$\times t$

For a replacement, the net operation cash flow will be:

Net Operation Cash flow $=[$ (Δrevenue$-\Delta$cost$-\Delta$depreciation)(1$-t$)$]+\Delta$depreciation[③]

$\qquad = $ (Δrevenue$-\Delta$cost)(1$-t$)$+\Delta$depreciation$\times t$

Example: Extending the earlier example, suppose that purchasing the machine is expected to reduce salaries by \$10000 per year and fringe benefits by \$1000 annually. In addition, the cost of defects will fall from \$8000 per year to \$3000. However, maintenance expenses will increase by \$4000 annually.

The annual depreciation on this new machine is \$7000 per year, whereas the depreciation expense lost with the sale of the old machine is \$2000 for each of the next five years. Annual depreciation on the new machine is calculated using the simplified straight-line method just described, that is taking the cost of the new machine plus any expenses necessary to put it in operating order and dividing by its depreciable life.

For this example, Table 7-6 shows the determination of the differential cash flows on an after-tax basis. Thus, the differential cash flows over the project's life are \$9200.

---

① The sale of the old machine is \$15000. This somewhat offsets the cash outflow.

②③ This non-cash item should be added back to reflect the true cash flow of the operating.

Table 7-6 Calculation of Differential Cash Flows for the Problem

	Book profit ($)	Cash flow ($)
Savings: Reduced salary	10000	10000
Reduced fringe benefits	1000	1000
Reduced defects ($8000- $3000)	5000	5000
Costs: Increased maintenance expense	-4000	-4000
Increased depreciation expense		
($7000- $2000)	-5000	0
Net savings before taxes	7000	12000
Taxes (40%)	-2800	-2800
Net operation cash flow after taxes		9200

(3) Terminal Cash Flows (终结现金流量).

At the end of the asset's life, there are certain cash inflows that occur. These are the after-tax salvage value and return of the net working capital.

Example: Somy Inc. would like to set up a new plant (expand). Currently, Somy has an option to buy an existing building at a cost of $25000. Necessary equipment for the plant will cost $15000, including installation costs.

The project would also require an initial investment of $10000 in net working capital (NWC). The project's estimated economic life is four years. At the end of that time, the building is expected to have a market value of $15000 and a book value of $22000, whereas the equipment would have a market value of $4000 and a book value of $2000.

Annual sales will be $80000. The production department has estimated that variable manufacturing costs would total 60 percent of sales and that fixed overhead costs, excluding depreciation, would be $10000 a year. The pre-tax depreciation for the building and equipment is:

Year 1 = $3000; year 2 = $6000; year 3 = $4000; year 4 = $3000.

Somy's marginal tax rate is 40 percent; its cost of capital is 12 percent; the firm's maximum acceptable payback period is 5 years.

Compute the initial investment outlay, operating cash flow over the project's life, and the terminal cash flows for Somy's expansion project. Then, determine whether the project should be accepted using payback analysis.

Answer:

1) Initial investment outlay.

Initial investment outlay =price of building+price of equipment+ΔNWC

$$= \$ 25000+ \$ 15000+ \$ 10000= \$ 50000$$

2) Operating cash flows.

$$\text{cash flow}_t = (\text{revenue}_t - \text{cost}_t)(1-\text{tax rate}) + (\text{depreciation}_t)(\text{tax rate})$$

$$\text{cash flow}_1 = [(80000-80000\times60\% -10000)(1-40\%)] + (3000)(0.4)= 14400$$

$$\text{cash flow}_2 = 13200+(6000)(0.4)= 15600$$

$$\text{cash flow}_3 = 13200+(4000)(0.4)= 14800$$

$$\text{cash flow}_4 = 13200+(3000)(0.4)= 14400$$

3) Terminal cash flows.

There are two elements to the terminal cash flow: return of net working capital, and salvage value. These are computed in Table 7-7.

Table 7-7　Terminal Cash Flow（$）

return of net-working capital		10000①
salvage value: building		15000②
book value of building	22000	
loss (22000-15000)	7000	

---

①　In this example, the initial NWC was negative, so the terminal value effect will be positive.
②　The sale of the building results in a cash inflow.

Continued

tax reduction from loss:		
(7000×0.4)		2800①
salvage value: equipment		4000
book value of equipment	2000	
gain (4000−2000)	2000	
taxes (2000×0.4)		−800
Net terminal year cash flow		31000
Operating cash flow in year 4		14400
Total cash flow in year 4		45400

The payback period for Somy's expansion project is computed as follows.

Cash Flow in Year 1: 50000−14400=35600

Year 2: 35600−15600=20000

Year 3: 20000−14800=5200

Payback period=3+ (5200/45400) = 3.11 years

Since 3.11 years<max payback 5 years, Somy should accept the project.

Replacement project analysis occurs when a firm must decide whether to replace an existing asset with a newer or better asset. In a replacement decision, cash flows from the old asset must be considered. Study the following example to understand the analysis.

Example: Suppose Somy wants to replace an existing printer with a new high-speed copier. The existing printer was purchased 10 years ago at a cost of $15000.

The printer had an expected life of 15 years, and the expected salvage value at the end of its life is zero. The printer is being depreciated on a straight-line basis. Currently, the printer has a book value of $5000.

The new high-speed copier can be purchased for $24000 (inclu-

---

① The building was sold for less than its book value. The loss on the building reduces taxes and results in a positive cash flow equal to the tax savings.

ding freight and installation). Over its 5-year life, it will reduce labor and raw materials usage sufficiently to cut annual operating costs from $14000 to $8000.

It is estimated that the new copier can be sold for $4000 at the end of five years; this is its estimated salvage value. The old printer's actual current market value is $2000, which is below its $5000 book value.

If the new copier is acquired, the old printer will be sold to another company rather than exchanged for the new copier. The company's marginal tax rate is40 percent. Net working capital requirements will also increase by $2000 at the time of replacement. The project's cost of capital is set at 11.5 percent.

The pre-tax depreciation for the equipment is:

Year 1 = $7920; year 2 = $10800; year 3 = $3600; year 4 = $1680; year 5 = $0.

Compute the initial investment outlay, operating cash flow over the project's life, and the terminal cash flows for Somy's replacement project. Then, determine whether the project should be accepted using NPV analysis.

Answer:

1) Initial investment outlay.

Assuming the old printer is sold, the adjustment for the sale is computed as:

Sale of old printer		$2000
Book value:	$5000	
Loss ($5000-$2000)	$3000	
Tax savings ($3000×0.4)		$1200
After-tax salvage value		$3200

$3200 must be treated as a cash inflow and reflected in the initial outlay.

$$\text{Net initial cash outflow} = -\text{cost} - \Delta \text{NWC} + \text{net inflow}$$
$$= -24000 - 2000 + 3200$$
$$= -\$22800$$

2) Operating cash flows.

When calculating depreciation for a replacement project, we need to decease the new printer depreciation expense by the depreciation that would have occurred with the old printer. Use the change in depreciation that occurs if the replacement is made.

$$\text{cash flow}_t = [\Delta\text{revenue} - \Delta\text{costs}](1 - \text{tax rate}) + (\Delta\text{ depreciation}_t)(\text{tax rate})$$

$$\text{cash flow}_1 = [0 - (-6000)(0.6)] + (7920 - 1000)(0.4) = 6368$$

$$\text{cash flow}_2 = [0 - (-6000)(0.6)] + (10800 - 1000)(0.4) = 7520$$

$$\text{cash flow}_3 = [0 - (-6000)(0.6)] + (3600 - 1000)(0.4) = 4640$$

$$\text{cash flow}_4 = [0 - (-6000)(0.6)] + (1680 - 1000)(0.4) = 3872$$

$$\text{cash flow}_5 = [0 - (-6000)(0.6)] + (0 - 1000)(0.4) = 3200$$

3) Terminal cash flow.

salvage value on new copier	4000
tax on salvage (4000) (0.4)	-1600[1]
return of net working capital	2000
cash flow$_5$	3200
Terminal year net cash flow	**7600**

GivenSomy's incremental cash flows and a cost of capital of 11.5 percent, net present value for the project can be computed as:

$$NPV = -22800 + \frac{6368}{1.115^1} + \frac{7520}{1.115^2} + \frac{4640}{1.115^3} + \frac{3872}{1.115^4} + \frac{7600}{1.115^5} = -778$$

Since the NPV is negative, Somy should not replace the printer with the new copier.

7.3   Decision Trees (决策树)

Sometimes projects can be structured so that expenditures do not have to be made all at one time, but rather can be made in stages over a period of years. This reduces

---

① Book value will be zero, resulting in a 4000 gain.

risk by giving managers the opportunity to reevaluate decisions using new information and then either investing additional funds or terminating the project. Such projects can be evaluated using decision trees.

Suppose a company is consideringa medicine program. The net investment for this project can be broken down into stages, as set forth in Figure 7-7. The company will do as follows.

Stage 1: at t = 0, which in this case is sometimes in the near future, conduct a $ 500000 study of the market potential.

Stage 2: if it appears that a sizable market does exist, then at t = 1, spend $ 1000000 to design and produce some samples. This medicine would then be evaluated by doctors and their reactions would determine whether the firm should proceed with the project.

Stage 3: if reaction to the medicine is good, then at t = 2, produce it at a net cost of $ 10000000. If this stage were reached, the project would generate either high or low net cash flows over the following two years.

A decision tree such as the one in Figure 7-7 can be used to analyze such multi-stage or sequential decisions. Here we assume that one year goes by between decisions.

Each circle represents a decision point, and it is called a decision node. The dollar value to the left of each decision node represents the net investment required at that decision point, and the cash flows shown under t = 3 to t = 4 represent the cash inflows if the project is pushed on to completion. Each diagonal line represents a branch of the decision tree, and each branch has an estimated probability.

For example, if the firm decides to "go" with the project at decision point 1, it will spend $ 500000 on a marketing study. Management estimates that there is a 0. 8 probability that the study will produce favorable results, leading to the decision to move on to stage 2, and a 0. 2 probability that the marketing study will produce negative results, indicating that the project should be canceled after stage 1. If the project is canceled, the cost to the company will be $ 500000 for the initial marketing study, and it will be a loss.

Based on the expectations set forth in Figure 7-7 and a cost of capital of 12 percent, the project's expected NPV is- $ 1. 043 million.

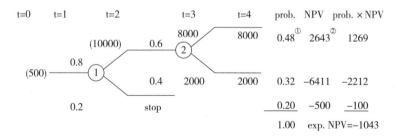

Figure 7-7 Decision Tree Analysis (in Thousands of Dollars)

---

① 0. 8×0. 6=0. 48.

② $\dfrac{8000}{1.\,12^3}+\dfrac{8000}{1.\,12^2}+\dfrac{-10000}{1.\,12^1}-500=2643.$

Experiment 7
Excel Implementation for NPV

用 Excel 解决净现值（NPV）问题

例：某项目初始投资 400000 元，在未来的第 1 年末、第 2 年末、第 3 年末、第 4 年末、第 5 年末均会收入 100000 元，若资金成本率为 10%，则该项目的净现值是多少（见表 7-8）？

表 7-8　求解 NPV

	A	B	C	D	E	F	G
1							
2		Discount Rate	10%				
3		Net Present Value	−20921.32	→	=C6+NPV(C2,C7:C11)		
4							
5		Year	Cash Flow				
6		0	−400000.00				
7		1	100000.00				
8		2	100000.00				
9		3	100000.00				
10		4	100000.00				
11		5	100000.00				

Experiment 8
Excel Implementation for IRR

例：某项目初始投资额为 400000 元，在未来的第 1 年末、第 2 年末、第 3 年末、第 4 年末、第 5 年末，均会收入现金流 100000 元，则项目的内部收益率是多少？

（1）直接使用 IRR 函数解决内部收益率问题（见表 7-9）。

表 7-9　直接使用 IRR

	A	B	C	D	E
1					
2		IRR		7.93%		
3					=IRR(C5:C10)	
4		Year	Cash Flow		
5		0	−400000.00		
6		1	100000.00		
7		2	100000.00		
8		3	100000.00		
9		4	100000.00		
10		5	100000.00		

（2）试错法。

使用 Excel 中的 Goal Seek 功能（工具栏—数据—模拟分析—规划求解）求解 IRR（见表 7-10）。

表 7-10　使用 Excel 中的 Goal Seek 功能

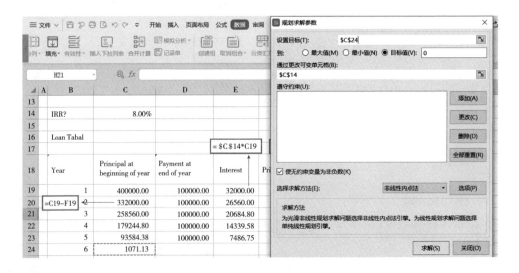

注：如果 C14 单元格的数值为 IRR的话，C24 单元格的值就应该呈现 0。设置目标"＄C＄24"，目标值为"0"，通过更改可变单元格"＄C＄14"，求解结果即为IRR。

Continued

	A	B	C	D	E	F
14		IRR?	7.93%			
15						
16		Loan Tabal				
17					= $C$14*C19	=D19–E19
18		Year	Principal at beginning of year	Payment at end of year	Interest	Principal
19		1	400000.00	100000.00	31723.30	68276.70
20	=C19–F19	2	331723.30	100000.00	26308.40	73691.60
21		3	258031.70	100000.00	20464.05	79535.95
22		4	178495.75	100000.00	14156.19	85843.81
23		5	92651.94	100000.00	7348.06	92651.94
24		6	0.00			
25						

本章小结

一、本章要点与难点

（1）资本预算决策方法。

投资回收期法

贴现的投资回收期法

净现值法

内部收益率法

修正的内部收益率法

（2）项目现金流预测法。

初始现金流＝投入成本－净流动资产投入＋旧设备处置现金流入＋/－旧设备处置相关税收

经营中现金流＝［（新增收入－新增成本－新增折旧）（1－税率）］＋新增折旧

末期现金流＝新设备处置现金流入＋/－新设备处置相关税收＋初期净流动资产投入偿还

二、Self-Test Problems

7-1　A company is considering the purchase of a copier that costs ＄5000. Assume a cost of capital of 10 percent and the following cash flow schedule：

Year 1：$ 3000

Year 2：$ 2000

Year 3：$ 2000

a. What is the project's payback period?

b. What is the project's discounted payback period?

c. What is the project's NPV?

d. What is the project's IRR?

7-2 An analyst has gathered the following data about Project A and B in a company with a 12 percent cost of capital (see Table 7-11).

a. If the projects are independent, which one should the company choose?

b. If the projects are mutually exclusive, what should the company do?

Table 7-11　Project A and B in a Company

	Project A	Project B
Initial cost	$ 15000	$ 20000
Life	5 years	4 years
Cash inflows	$ 5000/ year	$ 7500/ year

7-3 Given the following information, what is the initial cash outflow?

Purchase price of the new machine	$ 8000
Shipping and installation charge	2000
Sale price of old machine	6000
Book value of old machine	2000
Inventory increases if the new machine is installed	3000
Accounts payable increase if the new machine is installed	1000
Tax rate	25%

7-4 Jasic Inc. is evaluating two mutually exclusive investment projects. Assume both projects can be repeated indefinitely. Printer A has an NPV of $ 20000 over a 3-year life, and Printer B has a NPV of $ 25000 over a 5-year life. The project types are equally risky, and the firm's cost of capital is 12 percent. What is the equivalent annual annuity (EAA) of project A and B?

Chapter 8
Valuation of Securities
（证券估值）

8.1 Valuation of Bond （债券估值）

A bond is a long term contract under which a borrower agrees to make payments of interest and principal on specific dates to the holders of the bond. To understand bonds, it is important that you understand the following terms.

8.1.1 Par Value （面值）

The par value is the stated face value of the bond, it is generally represents the amount of money the firm borrows and promises to repay on the maturity date.

8.1.2 Coupon Rate （息票率）

The issuing company is required to pay a fixed number of interest each year (or, more typically, every six months). When this coupon payment, as it is called, is divided by the par value, the result is the coupon rate. For example, Somy's bonds have a $1000 par value, and they pay $100 as interest each year. The bond's coupon interest is $100, so its coupon rate is $100/$1000＝10%. This payment, which is fixed at the time the bond is issued, remains in force during the life of the bond.

In some cases, a bond's couponpayment will vary over time. For these floating rate bonds, the coupon rate is set for, say, the initial six-month period, after which it is adjusted every six months based on some market rate. Some bonds pay no coupons at all, but are offered at a substantial discount below their par values and hence provide capital appreciation rather than interest income. These securities are called zero coupon bonds.

8.1.3 Maturity Date (期限)

Bonds generally have a specified maturity date on which the par value must be repaid. Somy's bonds, which were issued on January 32007, will mature on January 32017; thus, they had a 10-year maturity at the time they were issued. Most bonds have original maturities ranging from 10 to 40 years. Of course, the effective maturity of a bond declines each year after it has been issued. Thus, Somy's bonds had a 10-year original maturity, but in 2008, a year later, they would have a 9-year maturity, and so on.

8.1.4 Provisions to Call or Redeem Bonds (赎回条款)

Most corporate bonds contain a call provision, which gives the issuing corporation the right to call the bonds for redemption.

The call provision generally states that the company must pay the bondholders an amount greater than the par value if they are called. The additional sum, which is termed a call premium, is often set equal to one year's interest if the bonds are called during the first year, and the premium declines at a constant rate of INT/N each year thereafter, where INT = annual interest, and N = original maturity in years.

For example, the call premium on a $1000 par value, 10-year, 10 percent bond would generally be $100 if it were called during the first year, $90 during the second year (calculated by reducing the $100 or 10% premium by one-tenth), and so on.

However, bonds are often not callable until several years (generally 5 to 10) after they were issued. This is known as a deferred call, and the bonds are said to have call protection.

8.1.5　Bond Valuation

The value of any financial asset is simply the present value of the cash flows the asset is expected to produce.

Therefore, a basic security valuation model can be defined mathematically as follows:

$$V = \frac{C_1}{(1+r)^1} + \frac{C_2}{(1+r)^2} + \cdots + \frac{C_n}{(1+r)^n}$$

$$V = \sum_{t=1}^{n} \frac{C_t}{(1+r)^t} \tag{8-1}$$

Where:

C_t = cash flow to be received at time t

V = the intrinsic value or present value of an asset producing expected future cash flows, C_t, in years 1 through n

r = the investor's required rate of return

Using the equation, there are three basic steps in the valuation process:

Step 1: estimate C_t which is the amount and timing of the future cash flows the security is expected to provide.

Step 2: determine r, the investor's required rate of return.

Step 3: calculate the intrinsic value, V, as the present value of expected future cash flows discounted at the investor's required rate of return.

Example: Consider a bond issued by Somy Inc. with a maturity date of 2016 and a stated coupon rate of 9 percent. In 1996, with 20 years left to maturity, investors owning the bonds required an 8.4 percent rate of return. Please calculate the value of the bonds to these investors using the following three-step valuation procedure.

Answer:

Step 1: estimate the amount and timing of the expected future cash flows.

Two types of cash flows are received by the bondholder:

a. Annual interest payments equal to the coupon rate of interest times the face value of the bond. In this example the bond's coupon interest rate is 9 percent; thus the annual interest payment is $90. Assuming that in 1996 interest payments have already been made, these cash flows will be received by the bondholder in each of the 20 years before the bond matures.

b. The face value of the bond of $1000 to be received in 2016.

Step 2: determine the investor's required rate of return by evaluating the riskiness of the bond's future cash flows. An 8.4 percent required rate of return for the bondholders is given.

Step 3: calculate the intrinsic value of the bond as the present value of the expected future interest and principal payments discounted at the investor's required rate of return.

The present value of somy's bonds is found as follows:

$$\text{Bond value} = V = \frac{\text{interest in year 1}}{(1+r)^1} + \frac{\text{interest in year 2}}{(1+r)^2} + \cdots +$$

$$\frac{\text{interest in year 20}}{(1+r)^{20}} + \frac{\text{par value of bond}}{(1+r)^{20}}$$

$$= \sum_{t=1}^{20} \frac{\text{interest in year } t}{(1+r)^t} + \frac{\text{par value of bond}}{(1+r)^{20}}$$

$$= \sum_{t=1}^{20} \frac{\$90}{(1+8.4\%)^t} + \frac{\$1000}{(1+8.4\%)^{20}}$$

$$= \$1057$$

8.1.6 Yield to Maturity (到期收益率)

Suppose you were offered a 14-year, 10 percent annual coupon, $1000 par value bond at a price of $1494.93. What rate of interest would you earn on your investment if you bought the bond and held it to maturity?

This rate is called the bond's yield to maturity (YTM), and it is the interest rate generally discussed by investors when they talk about rates of return. The yield to maturity is generally the same as the market rate of interest, r_d, and to find it, all you need to do is solve equation (8-1) for r_d:

$$V_B = \$1494.93 = \frac{\$100}{(1+r_d)^1} + \frac{\$100}{(1+r_d)^2} + \cdots + \frac{\$100}{(1+r_d)^{14}} + \frac{\$1000}{(1+r_d)^{14}}$$

You could substitute values for r_d until you find a value that "works" and force the sum of the PVs on the right side to equal $1494.93.

The yield to maturity can also be viewed as the bond's promised rate of return, which is the return that investors will receive if all the promised payments are made. However, the yield to maturity equals the expected rate of return only if the probability of default is zero and the bond cannot be called. If there is some default risk, or if the bond may be called, then there is some probability that the promised payments to maturity will not be received, in which case the calculated yield to maturity will differ from the expected return.

Note also that a bond's yield to maturity changes whenever interest rates in the economy change, and this is almost daily. One who purchases a bond and holds it until it matures will receive the YTM that exists on the purchase date, but the bond's calculated YTM will change frequently between the purchase date and the maturity date.

8.2   Valuation of Stock (股票估值)

In previous part we examined bonds. We now turn to common and preferred stock.

Valuing preferred stock is easy since the dividend is fixed and the income stream (dividends) is theoretically infinite (it is perpetuity):

$$\text{Preferred stock value} = \frac{D_P}{(1+r_P)^1} + \frac{D_P}{(1+r_P)^2} + \cdots + \frac{D_P}{(1+r_P)^\infty} = \frac{D_P}{r_P} \qquad (8-2)$$

Again, the only problem is determining the required rate of return, r_P. Because of default risk factors, the firm's required rate on preferred stock should be above the firm's bond rate.

Example: Preferred stock valuation

A company's bonds are currently yielding 8.5 percent, and its preferred shares are selling to yield 50 basis points (0.5 percent) below the firm's bond yield. Calculate the value of the company's 5 percent, $100 par value preferred stock.

Answer:

Determine the discount rate: $8.5\% - 0.5\% = 8.0\%$

Valuethe preferred stock: $\dfrac{D_P}{r_P} = \$5.00/0.08 = \$62.50$

Valuing common stock is more difficult than valuing bonds and preferred stock because the size and timing of future cash flows are uncertain, and the required rate of return on common equity, r_s, is unknown. However, a stock's value is still the PV of its future expected cash flows. Since the only cash flows stockholder ever receives from the firm are dividends, the model used is called the dividend discount model (DDM).

$$\text{Common stock value} = \frac{D_1}{(1+r_s)^1} + \frac{D_2}{(1+r_s)^2} + \cdots + \frac{D_\infty}{(1+r_s)^\infty} \qquad (8\text{-}3)$$

There are a couple of important comments that must be made here. First, if an investor sells the stock, the purchaser is buying the remaining dividend stream, so a stock's value at any point in time is still determined by the dividends it will pay after that point.

Second, if a company declares it will never pay dividends, its shares should be worthless because the stockholders would never receive anything of value from the firm. However, since we see shares of firms that pay no dividends being actively traded in the market, investors must expect to receive something of value, like a liquidation dividend, at some point in the future.

Steps used to determine a stock's value:

Step 1: Identify all expected future cash flows (dividends and future price).

Step 2: Estimate the equity discount rateke: $r_s = r_f + \beta(r_m - r_f)$.

Step 3: Discount the expected dividend and selling price at the required return.

8.2.1 One-Year Holding Period

If your holding period is one year, the value you will place on the stock today is the

PV of any dividends you will receive during the year plus the PV of the price you can sell the stock for at the end of the year. The valuation equation is:

$$\text{Value} = \frac{\text{dividend to be received}}{(1+r_s)^1} + \frac{\text{year-end price}}{(1+r_s)^1}$$

Example: One-period DDM valuation

Calculate the value of a stock that paid a \$1 dividend last year. You think next year's dividend will be 5 percent higher (g=0.05), and the stock will sell for \$12.80 at year end. The risk-free rate of interest is 6 percent, the market return is 12 percent, and the stock's β is 1.2.

Answer: The next dividend is the current dividend increased by the estimated growth rate. In this case, we have:

$$D_1 = D_0 \times (1+g) = 1.00 \times (1+0.05) = \$1.05$$

Next, we must estimatethe required return on equity. Using the CAPM we have:

$$r_s = r_f + \beta(r_m - r_f)$$
$$= 6.0\% + 1.2(12.0\% - 6.0\%)$$
$$= 13.2\%$$

Now, we can compute the present value of the expected future cash flows as follows:

$$V = \frac{\$1.05 + \$12.80}{(1+13.2\%)^1} = \$12.23$$

8.2.2 Multiple-year Holding Period

With a multiple-year holding period, we simply estimate all the dividends to be received as well as the expected selling price at the end of the holding period. For a 2-year holding period, we have:

$$\text{Value} = \frac{D_1}{(1+r_s)^1} + \frac{D_2}{(1+r_s)^2} + \frac{P_2}{(1+r_s)^2}$$

Example: Multiple-period DDM valuation

Using the stock in the preceding example, we had a current dividend of \$1.00, an expected growth rate of 5 percent, and the CAPM-determined required rate of return of 13. 2 percent. Calculate the value of this stock assuming that you expect to sell it for $14.00 in two years.

Answer:

$$PV = \frac{1.00 \times (1+0.05)}{(1+13.2\%)^1} + \frac{1.00 \times (1+0.05)^2}{(1+13.2\%)^2} + \frac{14.00}{(1+13.2\%)^2}$$
$$= \$12.71$$

8.2.3 Infinite Period

The infinite period DDM assumes the growth rate "g", in dividends from year to year is constant. Hence, next period's dividend, D_1, is $D_0(1+g_c)$, the second year's dividend, D_2, is $D_0(1+g_c)^2$, and so on, where g_c is a constant growth rate. The extended equation using this assumption is as follows:

$$V = \frac{D_0(1+g_c)}{(1+r_s)^1} + \frac{D_0(1+g_c)^2}{(1+r_s)^2} + \cdots + \frac{D_0(1+g_c)^\infty}{(1+r_s)^\infty} \tag{8-4}$$

This equation simplifies to:

$$V = \frac{D_0(1+g_c)}{r_s-g_c} = \frac{D_1}{r_s-g_c} \tag{8-5}$$

This is the infinite period dividend discount model.

Example: Infinite period DDM valuation

Calculate the value of a stock that paid a $2 dividend last year, if dividends are expected to grow at 5 percent forever. The risk-free rate is 6 percent; the expected return on the market is 11 percent; and the stock's beta is 1.2.

Answer:

Determine D_1: $D_1 = D_0(1+g_c) = \$2(1.05) = \$2.10$

Determine k_e: $r_s = r_f + \beta(r_m - r_f) = 0.06 + 1.2(0.11 - 0.06) = 12\%$

The stock's value $= \dfrac{D_0(1+g_c)}{r_s-g_c} = \dfrac{D_1}{r_s-g_c} = \$2.10/(0.12-0.05)$
$$= \$30.00$$

8.2.4　Multistage DDM

The infinite period DDM does not work with growth companies that can earn rates of return on investments that exceed the firm's cost of equity. This supernormal growth rate can even exceed the required rate of return on the firm's equity, but no firm can maintain this relationship indefinitely. We must assume the firm will return to a more sustainable rate of growth at some point in the future. Since the assumptions of the infinite period model ($r_s > g_c$) don't hold, the infinite period DDM cannot be used to value growth companies that are experiencing very rapid growth that will not continue forever.

A valuation approach for supernormal growth companies is to combine the multi-period and infinite period models. This is referred to as the multistage dividend discount model in many finance textbooks.

$$Value = \frac{D_1}{(1+r_s)^1} + \frac{D_2}{(1+r_s)^2} + \cdots + \frac{D_n}{(1+r_s)^n} + \frac{P_n}{(1+r_s)^n}$$

Where:

D_n = last dividend of the supernormal growth period

$P_n = \dfrac{D_{n+1}}{r_s - g_c}$, the first period's dividend after constant growth begins

D_{n+1} = first dividend affected by the constant growth rate, g_c

Steps in the temporary supernormal growth model are as follows.

Step1: project the supernormal dividend growth rate, $g_{supernormal}$.

Step2: using this supernormal growth rate, estimate dividends during the supernormal period.

Step3: forecast what the normal (constant) growth rate will be at the end of the supernormal growth period, g_c.

Step4: project the first dividend at the resumption of normal growth.

Step5: estimate the price of the stock at the end of the supernormal growth period.

Step6: determine thediscount rate, k_e.

Step7: add the PV of all dividends and the terminal stock price.

Example: Supernormal growth

Consider a stock with dividends that are expected to grow 20 percent per year for four years, after which they are expected to resume their normal growth rate of 5 percent per year, indefinitely. The last dividend paid was $1.00, and $r_s = 10$ percent. Calculate the value of this stock.

Answer:

Step 1: project the supernormal growth rate. (20% given)

Step 2: project dividends during the supernormal growth period using $g_{supernormal}$.

$$D_1 = D_0(1+g_{supernomal}) = 1.00(1.20) = \$1.20$$
$$D_2 = D_1(1+g_{supernomal}) = 1.20(1.20) = \$1.44$$
$$D_3 = D_2(1+g_{supernomal}) = 1.44(1.20) = \$1.73$$
$$D_4 = D_3(1+g_{supernomal}) = 1.73(1.20) = \$2.07$$

Step 3: forecast what the normal growth rate will be at the end of the supernormal growth period. (5% given)

Step 4: project the first dividend at the resumption of normal constant growth using g_c.

$$D_5 = D_4 (1+g_c) = 2.07 (1.05) = \$2.17$$

Step 5: find the price of the stock at the end of the supernormal growth period using the infinite period DDM.

$$P_4 = \frac{D_5}{r_s - g_c} = 2.18/ (0.10-0.05) = \$43.60$$

Step 6: determine the discount rate. (10% given)

Step 7: find PV of the cash stream at $r_s = 10\%$.

$$V = \frac{D_1}{(1+r_s)^1} + \frac{D_2}{(1+r_s)^2} + \frac{D_3}{(1+r_s)^3} + \frac{D_4}{(1+r_s)^4} + \frac{P_4}{(1+r_s)^4}$$
$$= \frac{1.20}{(1+0.10)^1} + \frac{1.44}{(1+0.10)^2} + \frac{1.73}{(1+0.10)^3} + \frac{2.07}{(1+0.10)^4} + \frac{43.60}{(1+0.10)^4}$$
$$= \$34.77$$

8.2.5 P/E Ratio (Price-to-Earning Ratio)

Now let's examine how does the DDM relate to the P/E ratio? Start with the general form of the infinite period DDM:

$$P_0 = \frac{D_1}{r_s - g}$$

Divide both sides of the equation by next year's projected earnings, E_1:

$$\frac{P_0}{E_1} = \frac{D_1 / E_1}{r_s - g}$$

This demonstrates that the P/E ratio is a function of:

$D_1 / E_1 =$ the expected dividend payout ratio.

$r_s =$ the required rate of return on the stock.

$g =$ the expected constant growth rate of dividends.

Example: P/E valuation method

A firm has an expected dividend payout ratio of 60 percent, a required rate or return of 11 percent, and an expected dividend growth rate of 5 percent. Calculate the firm's expected P/E ratio. If you expect next year's earnings to be $3.50, what is the value of the stock today?

Answer:

Step 1: estimate the expected P/E ratio:

$$\frac{P_0}{E_1} = \frac{D_1 / E_1}{r_s - g} = 0.6 / (0.11 - 0.05) = 10$$

Step 2: estimate the value of the stock:

$$P_0 = (E_1)(P_0 / E_1) = (\$3.50)(10) = \$35.00$$

8.2.6 About g

Assuming past investments are stable and dividends are calculated to allow for maintenance of past earnings power, the firm's earnings growth rate, g, can be defined as the firm's earnings plowback or retention rate (RR) times the return on the equity (ROE) portion of new investments.

$$g = (RR)(ROE)$$

Note that if RR is the earnings retention rate, $(1-RR)$ must be the firm's dividend payout rate.

Example: Assume ROE is constant and that new funds come solely from earnings retention. Calculate the firm's growth rate, given that the firm earns 10 percent on equity of $100 per share and pays out 40 percent of earnings in dividends.

Answer：

$$g=(\text{ROE})(\text{RR})=(0.10)(1-0.40)=6\%$$

本章小结

一、本章要点与难点

（1）债券估值：$V=\sum_{t=1}^{n}\dfrac{C_t}{(1+r)^t}$

（2）股票估值。

优先股：$V=\dfrac{D_P}{(1+r_P)^1}+\dfrac{D_P}{(1+r_P)^2}+\cdots+\dfrac{D_P}{(1+r_P)^\infty}=\dfrac{D_P}{r_P}$

普通股：$V=\dfrac{D_1}{(1+r_s)^1}+\dfrac{D_2}{(1+r_s)^2}+\cdots+\dfrac{D_\infty}{(1+r_s)^\infty}$

二、Self-Test Problems

8-1 Machines Unlimited shares are expected to pay dividends of $1.55 and $1.72 at the end of each of the next two years, respectively. The investor expects the price of the shares at the end of this 2-year holding period to be $42.00. The investor's required rate of return is 14 percent. Calculate the current value of Machines Unlimited shares.

8-2 Downa Company recently paid a dividend of $1.80. An analyst has examined the financial statements and historical dividend policy of Downa and expects that the firm's dividend rate will grow at a constant rate of 3.5 percent indefinitely. The analyst also determines Downa's beta is1.5, the risk free rate is 4 percent, and the expected return on the market portfolio is 8 percent. Calculate the current value of Downa's shares?

8-3 Allice Inc. currently pays a dividend of $1.50. An analyst forecasts growth of 10 percent for the next three years, followed by 4 percent growth in perpetuity thereafter. The required return is 12 percent. Calculate the current value per share.

Part Four

Financial Analysis
(财务分析)

Chapter 9
Analysis of Financial Statements
(财务报表分析)

The purpose of this part is to introduce you to the basics of financial statement analysis. Financial statement analysis is a key element in corporate finance. Analysts review a company's financial statements to gain insight into the firm's financial decision-making and operating performance. Usually, financial data is converted into ratios to make them meaningful and easier to analyze. Although there are literally dozens of ratios that can be computed, there is a relatively small subset that provides an analyst with most of the relevant information about a firm.

When performing analysis with financial ratios, it is important to remember that:

A single value of a financial ratio is notmeaningful by itself, it must be examined in context of the firm's history, the industry, the major competitors, and the economy.

Ratios by themselves don't answer the analyst's questions. Rather, ratios are designed to provide the analyst with pertinentquestions to assist in conducting the analysis of the firm.

Commonly, ratios can be used to evaluate four different facets of a company's performance and condition: ①internal liquidity, ②operating performance, ③risk profile, ④growth potential.

9.1 Internal Liquidity Ratios (偿债能力比率)

Liquidity ratios are employed by analysts to determine the firm's ability to pay its short-term liabilities.

The current ratio is the best known measure of liquidity:

$$\text{Current ratio（流动比率）} = \frac{\text{current assets}}{\text{current liabilities}} \qquad (9\text{-}1)$$

The higher the current ratio, the more likely the company will be able to pay its short term bills. A current ratio of less than one means that the company has negative working capital and is probably facing a liquidity crisis.

The quick ratio is a more stringent measure of liquidity because it does not include inventories and other assets that might not be very liquid:

$$\text{Quick ratio（速动比率）} = \frac{\text{cash+marketable securities+receivables}}{\text{current liabilities}} \qquad (9\text{-}2)$$

The higher the quick ratio, the more likely the company will be able to pay its short term bills.

The most conservative liquidity measure is the cash ratio:

$$\text{Cash ratio（现金比率）} = \frac{\text{cash+marketable securities}}{\text{current liabilities}} \qquad (9\text{-}3)$$

The higher the cash ratio, the more likely the company will be able to pay its short term bills.

The current, quick, and cash ratios differ only in the assumed liquidity of the current assets that the analyst projects will be used to pay off current liabilities.

A measure of accounts receivable liquidity is the receivables turnover ratio:

$$\text{Receivables turnover ratio（应收账款周转率）} = \frac{\text{net annual sales}}{\text{average receivables}} \text{①} \quad (9\text{-}4)$$

It is considered desirable to have a receivables turnover figure close to the industry norm.

The inverse of the receivables turnover times 365 is the average collection period, which is the average number of days it takes for the company's customers to pay their bills:

---

① Averages are calculated by adding the beginning of year account value and the end of year account value, then dividing the sum by two.

Average receivables collection period（应收账款周转期）

$$= \frac{365}{\text{receivables turnover}} \tag{9-5}$$

It is considered desirable to have a collection period close to the industry norm. A collection period that is too high might mean that customers are too slow in paying their bills, which means too much capital is tied up in assets. A collection period that is too low might indicate that the firm's credit policy is too rigorous, which might hamper sales.

A measure of a firm's efficiency with respect to its processing and inventory management is the inventory turnover ratio:

$$\text{Inventory turnover ratio（存货周转率）} = \frac{\text{cost of goods sold}}{\text{average inventory}} \tag{9-6}$$

The inverse of the inventory turnover times 365 is the average inventory processing period:

Average inventory processing period（存货周转期）

$$= \frac{365}{\text{inventory turnover}} \tag{9-7}$$

As is the case with accounts receivable, it is considered desirable to have an inventory processing period close to the industry norm. A processing period that is too high might mean that too much capital is tied up in inventory and could mean that the inventory is obsolete. A processing period that is too low might indicate that the firm has inadequate stock on hand, which could adversely impact sales.

A measure of the use of trade credit by the firm is the payables turnover ratio:

$$\text{Payables turnover ratio（应付账款周转率）} = \frac{\text{cost of goods sold}}{\text{average trade payables}} \tag{9-8}$$

The inverse of the payables turnover ratio multiplied by 365 is the payables payment period, which is the average amount of time it takes the company to pay its bills:

$$\text{Payables payment period（应付账款周转期）} = \frac{365}{\text{payables turnover ratio}} \tag{9-9}$$

The cash conversion cycle（现金周转期）is the length of time it takes to turn the firm's investment into cash, which is used to create inventory back into cash in the form of collections from the sales of that inventory. The cash conversion cycle is computed from days of receivables, days of inventory, and the payables payment period.

$$\text{Cash conversion cycle} = \begin{bmatrix} \text{average receivables} \\ \text{collection period} \end{bmatrix} + \begin{bmatrix} \text{average inventory} \\ \text{processing period} \end{bmatrix} - \begin{bmatrix} \text{payables payment} \\ \text{period} \end{bmatrix}$$

$$(9-10)$$

High cash conversion cycles are considered undesirable. A conversion cycle that is too high implies that the company has an excessive amount of capital investment in the sales process.

9.2   Ratios Evaluating Operating Performance (营运能力指标)

Operating performance ratios help determine how well management operates the business. They can be divided into two categories: operating efficiency ratios and operating profitability ratios.

Operating efficiency ratios are comprised of the total asset turnover, net fixed asset turnover, and equity turnover ratios. These are the first three ratios presented.

Operating profitability ratios include the gross profit margin, operating profit margin, net profit margin, return on total capital, and return on total equity and so on. Operating ratios compare the top line of the income statement to profits.

The effectiveness of the firm's use of its total assets to create revenue is measured by the ratio of total asset turnover:

$$\text{Total asset turnover （总资产周转率）} = \frac{\text{net sales}}{\text{average total net assets}} \quad (9-11)$$

Different types of industries might have considerably different turnover ratios. Manufacturing businesses that are capital intensive might have asset turnover ratios near one, while retail businesses might have turnover ratios near 10.

The utilization of fixed assets is measured by the net fixed asset turnover:

$$\text{Fixed asset turnover （固定资产周转率）} = \frac{\text{net sales}}{\text{average net fixed assets}} \quad (9-12)$$

As was the case withthe total asset turnover ratio, it is desirable to have a fixed asset turnover close to the industry norm. Low fixed asset turnover might mean that the company has too much capital tied up in its asset base. A turnover ratio that is too high might imply that the firm has obsolete equipment, or at a minimum, the firm will probably have to incur capital expenditures in the near future to increase capacity to support growing revenues.

The equity turnover is a measure of the employment of owner's capital:

$$\text{Equity turnover (净资产周转率)} = \frac{\text{net sales}}{\text{average equity}} \qquad (9\text{-}13)$$

For this ratio, equity capital includes all preferred and common stock, paid-in capital, and retained earnings, although some analysts use only common equity, which excludes preferred stock. Analysts need to consider the capital structure of the company in evaluating this ratio because a company can increase this ratio without increasing profitability simply by using more debt financing.

Operating profitability ratios examine how good the management is at turning their efforts into profits.

Know these terms and their relevance first:

Net sales

- Cost of goods sold

  Gross profit

- Operating expenses

  Operating profit (EBIT)

- Interest

  Earnings before taxes (EBT)

- Taxes

  Earnings after taxes (EAT) or net income

The gross profit margin is the ratio of gross profit to sales:

$$\text{Gross profit margin (毛利润率)} = \frac{\text{gross profit}}{\text{net sales}} \qquad (9\text{-}14)$$

An analyst should be concerned if this ratio is too low.

The operating profit margin is the ratio of operating profit to sales. Operating profit is also referred to as earnings before interest and taxes.

$$\text{Operating profit margin (经营利润率)} = \frac{\text{operating profit}}{\text{net sales}} = \frac{\text{EBIT}}{\text{net sales}} \qquad (9\text{-}15)$$

Some analysts prefer to calculate the operating profit margin by adding back depreciation expense to arrive at earnings before depreciation, interest, taxes, and amortization (EBDITA).

The net profit margin is the ratio of net income to sales:

$$\text{Net profit margin（净利润率）} = \frac{\text{net income}}{\text{net sales}} \qquad (9-16)$$

Analysts should be concerned if this ratio is too low.

The return on total capital is the ratio of net income plus interest expense to total capital:

$$\text{Return on total capital（资产报酬率）} = \frac{\text{net income+interest expense}}{\text{average total capital}} \quad (9-17)$$

Total capital is the same as total assets. The interest expense that should be added back is gross interest expense, not net interest expense (which is gross interest expense minus interest income).

The return on total equity is the ratio of net income to total equity (including preferred stock):

$$\text{Return on total equity（净资产报酬率）} = \frac{\text{net income}}{\text{average total equity}} \qquad (9-18)$$

Analysts should be concerned if this ratio is too low.

A similar ratio to the return on total equity is the return on owner's equity:

$$\text{Return on common equity} = \frac{\text{net income-preferred dividends}}{\text{average common equity}} \qquad (9-19)$$

This ratio differs from the return on total equity in that it only measures the accounting profits available to, and the capital invested by, common stockholders, instead of common and preferred stockholders. That is why preferred dividends are deducted from net income in the numerator. Analysts should be concerned if this ratio is too low. And this ratio is what we commonly called ROE (return on equity).

The return on common equity is often more thoroughly analyzed using the DuPont (杜邦) decomposition.

The DuPont system of analysis is an approach that can be used to analyze return on equity. It uses basic algebra to breakdown ROE into a function of different ratios, so an analyst can see the impact of leverage, profit margins, and turnover on shareholders' returns. There are two variants of the DuPont system: the original three part approach and the extended five part system.

In the original approach, ROE is defined as:

$$\text{Return on equity} = \frac{\text{net income}}{\text{equity}} \qquad (9\text{-}20)$$

Note that there are two subtle differences between this ROE measure and the ROE defined previously. First, the numerator does not subtract preferred dividends as our review did when ROE was first defined. Second, the common equity figure that is used in this ROE is not average equity, but simply end-of-year equity.

Multiplying ROE by sales/sales and rearranging terms produce:

$$\text{Return on equity} = \frac{\text{net income}}{\text{sales}} \times \frac{\text{sales}}{\text{equity}} \qquad (9\text{-}21)$$

The first term is the profit margin and the second term is the equity turnover, so we rewrite (9-21) as:

$$\text{Return on equity} = \text{net profit margin} \times \text{equity turnover} \qquad (9\text{-}22)$$

We can expand this further by multiplying these terms by assets/assets, and rearranging terms:

$$\text{Return on equity (ROE)} = \frac{\text{net income}}{\text{sales}} \times \frac{\text{sales}}{\text{assets}} \times \frac{\text{assets}}{\text{equity}} \qquad (9\text{-}23)$$

The first term is still the profit margin, the second term is now asset turnover, and the third term is now an equity multiplier that will increase as the use of debt financing increases, so (9-23) can be written as:

$$\text{Return on equity} = \text{net profit margin} \times \text{asset turnover} \times \text{equity multiplier} \qquad (9\text{-}24)$$

This is the original DuPont equation. Since it beaks down a very important ratio into three key components, if ROE is low, we can find the reason that at least one of the following is true: the company has a poor profit margin, the company has poor asset turnover, or the firm has little leverage.

Example: A company has a profit margin of 4 percent, asset turnover of 2.0, and a debt-to-assets ratio of 60 percent. What is the ROE?

Answer: Debt-to-assets = 60%, which means equity to assets is 40%; this also implies that assets-over-equity of 1/0.4 = 2.5.

$$\text{ROE} = \frac{\text{net income}}{\text{sales}} \times \frac{\text{sales}}{\text{assets}} \times \frac{\text{assets}}{\text{equity}} = \text{net profit margin} \times \text{asset turnover} \times$$

equity multiplier

$$= (0.04)(2.00)(2.50) = 20\%$$

The extended DuPont equation takes the net profit margin and breaks it down further. The numerator of the net profit margin is net income. Since net income is equal to earnings before taxes multiplied by 1 minus the tax rate $(1-t)$, the DuPont equation can be written as:

$$\text{ROE} = \frac{\text{earnings before tax}}{\text{sales}} \times \frac{\text{sales}}{\text{assets}} \times \frac{\text{assets}}{\text{equity}} \times (1-t) \qquad (9-25)$$

Earning-before-tax is simply EBIT minus interest expense. If this substitution is made, the equation becomes:

$$\text{ROE} = [\,(\frac{\text{EBIT}}{\text{sales}})(\frac{\text{sales}}{\text{assets}}) - (\frac{\text{interest expense}}{\text{assets}})\,] \times \frac{\text{assets}}{\text{equity}} \times (1-t) \qquad (9-26)$$

The first term is the operating profit margin. The second term is the asset turnover. The third term is new and is called the interest expense rate. The fourth term is the same leverage multiplier defined in the traditional DuPont equation, and the fifth term, $(1-t)$, is called the tax retention rate.

The equation can now be stated as:

$$\text{ROE} = \left[\begin{pmatrix}\text{operating} \\ \text{profit} \\ \text{margin}\end{pmatrix}\begin{pmatrix}\text{total} \\ \text{asset} \\ \text{turnover}\end{pmatrix} - \begin{pmatrix}\text{interest} \\ \text{expense} \\ \text{rate}\end{pmatrix}\right]\begin{pmatrix}\text{financial} \\ \text{leverage} \\ \text{multiplier}\end{pmatrix}\begin{pmatrix}\text{tax} \\ \text{retention} \\ \text{rate}\end{pmatrix} \qquad (9-27)$$

Note that in general, high profit margins, leverage, and asset turnover will lead to high levels of ROE. However, this version of the formula shows that more leverage does not always lead to higher ROE. As leverage rises, so does the interest expense rate. Hence, the positive effects of leverage can be offset by the higher interest payments that accompany more debt. Note that higher taxes will always lead to lower levels of ROE.

9.3 Other Useful Ratios (其他常用指标)

9.3.1 Ratios for Risk Analysis (风险测量指标)

Risk analysis calculations measure the uncertainty of the firm's income flows.

A measure of the firm's use of fixed cost financing sources is the debt-to-equity ratio:

$$\text{Debt-to-equity ratio (债权比率)} = \frac{\text{total long-term debt}}{\text{total equity}} \qquad (9-28)$$

Some analysts exclude preferred stock and only use owner's equity. Increases and decreases in this ratio suggest a greater or lesser reliance on debt as a source of financing.

Another way of looking at the usage of debt is the long-term debt-to-total-capital ratio:

$$\text{Long-term debt-to-total-capital} = \frac{\text{total long-term debt}}{\text{total long-term capital}} \qquad (9-29)$$

Total long-term capital equals all long-term debt plus preferred stock and equity. Increases and decreases in this ratio suggest a greater or lesser reliance on debt as a source of financing.

A slightly different way of analyzing debt utilization is the total debt ratio, which includes current liabilities in both the numerator and the denominator:

$$\text{Total debt ratio} = \frac{\text{current liabilites+total long-term debt}}{\text{total debt+total equity}} \qquad (9-30)$$

Increases and decreases in this ratio suggest a greater or lesser reliance on debt as a source of financing. Please note that total debt includes all liabilities, even accounts payable and deferred taxes, which are non-interest bearing accounts.

Often, only interest bearing debt and equity are considered to be long-term capital. A further refinement excludes accounts payable and accrued expenses, which may be considered part of the firm's working capital[①], to get the following relationship:

$$\left[\begin{array}{c}\text{Total interest-bearing debt}\\ \text{to total funded capital}\end{array}\right] = \frac{\text{total interest-bearing debt}}{\text{total capital-noninterest bearing liabilities}}$$

(9-31)

The remaining risk ratios help determine the firm's ability to repay its debt obligations. The first of these is the interest coverage ratio:

$$\text{Interest coverage （利息保障倍数）} = \frac{\text{earnings before interest and taxes}}{\text{interest expense}}$$ (9-32)

The lower this ratio, the more likely the firm will have difficulty meeting its debt payments.

9.3.2 Growth Analysis Ratios（成长能力指标）

Owners and creditors are interested in the firm's growth potential. Owners pay attention to growth because stock valuation is dependent on the future growth rate of the firm. The analysis of growth potential is important to the creditors because the firm's future prospects are crucial to its ability to pay existing debt obligations. If the company doesn't grow, it stands a much greater chance of defaulting on its loans. In theory, the growth rate of a firm, is a function of the rate of return earned on its resources and the amount of resources retained and reinvested.

To calculate the sustainable growth rate of a firm, the rate of return on resources is measured as the return on equity capital, or the ROE. The proportion of earnings reinvested is known as the retention rate (RR).

The formula for the sustainable growth rate, which is how fast the firm can grow without additional external equity issues while holding leverage constant, is:

$$g = RR \times ROE$$ (9-33)

The calculation of the retention rate is:

---

① Net working capital = current asset - current liabilities.

$$\text{Retention rate （留存比率）} = \left(1 - \frac{\text{dividends declared}}{\text{operating income after taxes}}\right) \quad (9-34)$$

Where:

$$\left(\frac{\text{dividends declared}}{\text{operating income after taxes}}\right) = \text{dividend payout ratio} \quad (9-35)$$

本章小结

一、本章要点与难点

（1）流动比率，速动比率，现金比率。

（2）存货周转率，存货周转周期。

（3）应收账款周转率，应收账款周转周期。

（4）毛利润率，净利润率，净资产报酬率。

（5）杜邦分析法。

$$\text{ROE} = \frac{\text{net income}}{\text{sales}} \times \frac{\text{sales}}{\text{assets}} \times \frac{\text{assets}}{\text{equity}}$$

$$\text{ROE} = \left[\left(\frac{\text{EBIT}}{\text{sales}}\right)\left(\frac{\text{sales}}{\text{assets}}\right) - \left(\frac{\text{interest expense}}{\text{assets}}\right)\right] \times \frac{\text{assets}}{\text{equity}} \times (1-t)$$

二、Self-Test Problems

9-1 A company has a net profit margin of 4 percent, an asset turnover of 2.0, and a debt-to-asset ratio of 60 percent. Calculate the ROE.

9-2 An analyst has gathered data from two companies in the same industry. Calculate the ROE for both companies using the extended DuPont equation, and explain the critical factors that can lead to a higher ROE (see Table 9-1).

Table 9-1 Selected Income and Balance Sheet Data ($)

	Company A	Company B
Revenues	500	900
Operating income	35	100

Continued

	Company A	Company B
Interest expense	5	0
Income before taxes	30	100
Taxes	10	40
Net income	20	60
Total assets	250	300
Total debt	100	50
Owners' equity	150	250

9-3   Table 9-2 shows a balance sheet for a company in 2018 and 2019. Table 9-3 shows its income statement in 2019. Using the company information in Table 9-2, Table 9-3, Table 9-4 calculates the current year ratios. Discuss how to use these ratios compare with the company's performance last year with the industry's performance.

Table 9-2   Balance Sheet 2018 and 2019（$）

Year	2019	2018
Assets		
Cash	105	95
Receivables	205	195
Inventories	310	290
Total current assets	620	580
Gross property, plant, and equipment (PP&E)	1800	1700
Accumulated depreciation	360	340
Net PP&E	1440	1360
Total assets	2060	1940
Liabilities		
Payables	110	90
Short-term debt	160	140
Current portion of long-term debt	55	45

Continued

Year	2019	2018
Total current liabilities	325	275
Long-term debt	610	690
Deferred taxes	105	95
Common stock	300	300
Additional paid-in capital	400	400
Retained earnings	320	180
Common shareholders equity	1020	880
Total liabilities and equity	2060	1940

Table 9-3　Income Statement of 2019 ($)

Year	2019
Sales	4000
Cost of goods sold	3000
Gross profit	1000
Operating expenses	650
Operating profit	350
Interest expense	50
Earnings before taxes	300
Taxes	100
Net income	200
Common dividends	60

Table 9-4　Financial Ratio Template

	Last year	Industry
Current ratio	2. 1	1. 5
Quick ratio	1. 0	0
Receivables collection period	18. 9	18. 0
Inventory turnover	10. 7	12. 0

Continued

	Last year	Industry
Total asset turnover	2. 3	2. 4
Equity turnover	4. 8	4. 0
Gross profit margin	27. 4%	29. 3%
Net profit margin	5. 8%	6. 5%
Return on capital	13. 3%	15. 6%
Return on equity	24. 1%	19. 8%
Debt-to-equity	78. 4%	35. 7%
Interest coverage	5. 9	9. 2
Retention rate	50. 0%	43. 6%
Sustainable growth rate	12. 0%	8. 6%

9-4　Complete the balance sheet and sales information in Table 9-5 by using the following financial data.

Debt ratio: 50%

Quick ratio: 0. 80

Total assets turnover: 1. 50

Receivables turnover: 10

Gross profit margin: 25%

Inventory turnover: 3. 75

Table 9-5　Balance Sheet（$）

Cash		Accounts payable	
Accounts receivable		Long-term debt	60000
Inventories		Common stock	
Fixed assets		Retained earnings	97500
Total assets	300000	Total liabilities and equity	
Sales		Cost of goods sold	

Chapter 10
Cash Flow Analysis
（现金流分析）

10.1 The Key Elements of CFO, CFI and CFF

Items on the cash flow statement come from two sources: ①income statement items, ②changes in balance sheet accounts.

The cash flow statement divides cash flow into three components.

Cash flow from operations (CFO, 经营性现金流) reports the cash generated from sales and the cash used in the production process. These items essentially flow through the firm's income statement and working capital accounts[①]. Its key elements are:

Cash collections from sales;

Cash inputs into the manufacturing or retail process;

Cash operating expenses;

Cash interest expense;

Cash tax payments.

Cash flow from investing (CFI, 投资性现金流) reports the cash used for property, plant, and equipment as well as investments, acquisitions; and the cash generated from sales of assets or businesses. These items are found in the non-current portion of the asset section of the balance sheet. Its key elements are:

Purchases of property, plant, and equipment;

---

① Working capital accounts are current assets and current liabilities.

Investments in joint ventures and affiliates;

Payments for businesses acquired;

Proceeds from sales of assets;

Investments (or sales of investments) in markeTable securities.

Cash flow from financing (CFF, 融资性现金流) reports capital structure transactions. These items are found in the long-term capital section of the balance sheet and the statement of retained earnings. Its key elements are:

Cash dividends paid;

Increases or decreases in short-term borrowings;

Long-term borrowings and repayment of long-term borrowings;

Stock sales and repurchases.

In most cases the classification of cash flows isstraightforward. Items that affect cash flow are either an income statement account or a change in a balance sheet account. As a general rule, an increase in an asset account or a decrease in a liability account requires the use of cash and, therefore, decreases the cash flow to the firm. For example, purchasing more inventories (increase in an asset account) or retiring trade credit (decrease in a liability) results in the use of cash and a decrease in cash flow. Likewise, a decrease in an asset account (or an increase in a liability account) represents a source of cash and an increase to the firm's cash flow.

Now, we go detailed to examine each of the cash flow.

Operating cash flows (CFO): All items affecting income are included in operating cash flow. And changes in asset or liability accounts that are results of the sales or production process also are classified as operating cash flows.

Examples of balance sheet items that are classified as operating cash flows include changes in:

Receivables;

Inventories;

Prepaid expenses;

Taxes, interest, and miscellaneous payables;

Deferred taxes.

Examples of income statement items that are classified as operating cash flows include:

Cash sales;

Cash cost of sales;

Cash general and administrative expenses;

Cash taxes;

Interest paid and received;

Dividends received.

Investing cash flows (CFI): Changes in asset accounts, typically long-term assets, which reflect capital investment in the company, are classified as investing cash flows. Examples of items that are classified as investing cash flows include changes in:

Most gross fixed-asset accounts;

Marke Table securities.

Financing cash flows (CFF): Changes in equity accounts, including dividends, and changes in liabilities that are part of the capital structure are classified as financing cash flows. Examples of items that are classified as financing cash flows include:

Dividends paid to the company's shareholders;

A change in liability accounts that represent financing (typically interest-bearing debt or deep-discounting debt);

A change in equity accounts.

Some transactions do not result in immediate cash inflows or cash outflows. These transactions are disclosed in footnotes. However, these transactions typically involve an investing and/or financing decision. For example, if a firm acquires a building or real estate by assuming a mortgage, the firm has made an investment and financing decision. Economically, this is equivalent to borrowing the purchase amount.

10.2 The Calculation of CFO, CFI and CFF

10.2.1 Calculate CFO

(1) Direct method.

The direct method presents operating cash flow by taking each item from the income statement and converting it to its cash equivalent by adding or subtracting the changes in the corresponding balance sheet accounts. Footnotes are often helpful in learning about how inflows and outflows have affected the balance sheet accounts.

(2) Indirect method.

The indirect method calculates cash flow operations in four steps:

Step 1: begin with net income.

Step 2: subtract gains or add losses that result from financing or investment cash flows (such as gains from sale of land).

Step 3: add back all non-cash charges to income (such as depreciation and goodwill amortization) and subtract all non-cash revenue components.

Step 4: add or subtract changes to operating accounts as follows.

Increase in the balances of operating asset accounts are subtracted, while decreases in those accounts are added.

Increases in the balances of operating liability accounts are added, while decreases are subtracted.

10.2.2　Calculate CFI

Investing cash flows (CFI) are calculated by finding the changes in the appropriate gross fixed-asset account. Changes in non-cash fixed-asset accounts, such as accumulated depreciation and goodwill, are not included since they do not represent a cash transaction. Any gains or losses from the disposal of an asset must also be reflected in cash flow.

Cash from asset disposal = decrease in asset+gain from sale

10.2.3　Calculate CFF

Financing cash flows are determined by measuring the cash flows occurring between the firm and its suppliers of capital. Cash flows between the firm and creditors result from new borrowings and debt repayments. Note, interest paid is technically a cash flow to the creditors but it is already accounted for in CFO. Cash flows between the firm and the shareholders or owners occur as equity issued, share repurchases, and dividends.

CFF is the sum of these two measures:

Net cash flows from creditors = new borrowings − principal repaid

Net cash flows from owners = new equity issued − share repurchases − cash dividends

Where:

Cash dividends are measured by using dividends paid and changes in dividends payable

CFF = net cash flows from creditors + net cash flows from owners

Finally, total cash flow is equal to the sum of cash flow from operations, cash flow from investments, and cash flow from financing. If done correctly, the total cash flow will equal the change in the cash balance from the beginning-of-period to the end-of-period balance sheet.

The following is the format of the basic statement of cash flows:

cash flow from operations (CFO) +

cash flow from investing (CFI) +

cash flow from financing (CFF)

change in the cash account+

beginning cash balance

ending cash balance

Example: Prepare a statement of cash flows using the direct method for a company with the following income statement and balance sheets. Keep track of the balance sheet items used to calculate CFO by marking them off the balance sheet (see Table 10-1, Table 10-2). They will not be needed again when determining CFI and CFF.

Table 10-1　Income Statement of 2018 ($)

Sales	100000
Cost of goods sold	40000
Wages	5000
depreciation	7000
interest	500
Total expenses	52500

	Continued
Sales	100000
Income from continuing operations	47500
Gain from sale of land	10000
Pretax income	57500
Provision for taxes	−20000
Net income	37500
Common dividends declared	8500

Table 10-2　Balance Sheet of 2018 and 2019 （$）

Balance sheet	2019	2018
Cash	33000	9000
Accounts receivable	10000	9000
Inventory	5000	7000
Current assets	48000	25000
Land	35000	40000
Gross plant and equipment	85000	60000
Accumulated depreciation	−16000	−9000
Net plant and equipment	69000	51000
Non-current assets	104000	91000
Goodwill	10000	10000
Total assets	162000	126000
Liabilities		
Accounts payable	9000	5000
Wages payable	4500	8000
Interest payable	3500	3000
Taxes payable	5000	4000
Dividends payable	6000	1000
Current liabilities	28000	21000

Balance sheet	2019	2018
Bonds	15000	10000
Deferred taxes	20000	15000
Common stock	40000	50000
Retained earnings	59000	30000
Non-current liabilities	35000	25000
Stockholders' equity	99000	80000
Total liabilities & stockholders' equity	162000	126000

Continued

Answer:

(1) Cash from operations.

1) Cash flow from operations (use the direct method).

Cash collections = net sales − increase in receivables

= \$100000 − \$1000 = \$99000

Cash inputs = − cost of goods sold + decrease in inventory + increase in accounts payable

= − \$40000 + \$2000 + \$4000 = − \$34000

Cash expenses = − wages − decrease in wages payable

= − \$5000 − \$3500 = − \$8500

Cash interest = − interest expense + increase in interest payable

= − \$500 + \$500 = 0

Cash taxes = − tax expense + increase in taxes payable + increase in deferred taxes

= − \$20000 + \$1000 + \$5000 = − \$14000

Cash flow from operation = \$99000 − \$34000 − \$8500 + 0 − \$14000

= \$42500

2) Cash flow from operations (use the indirect method).

Step 1: start with net income of \$37500.

Step 2: subtract gain from sale of land of \$10000.

Step 3: add back non-cash charges of depreciation of \$7000.

Step 4: subtract increases in receivables and inventories and add increases of payables and deferred taxes.

Net income	37500
−gain from sale of land	−10000
+depreciation	7000
subtotal	$ 34500
Changes in operating accounts	
−increase in receivables	−1000
+decrease in inventories	2000
+increase in accounts payable	4000
−decrease in wages payable	−3500
+increase in interest payable	500
+increase in taxes payable	1000
+increase in deferred taxes	5000
CFO	$ 42500

(2) Investing cash flow.

In this example, we have two components of investing cash flow: the sale of land and the change in gross property, plant and equipment (PP&E).

Cash from sale of land = decrease in asset + gain on sale

$$= \$ 5000 + \$ 10000 = \$ 15000 \text{ (source)}$$

Note: if the land had been sold at a loss, we would have subtracted the loss amount from the decrease in assets.

Change in gross PP&E = 2019 ending balance − 2018 ending balance

$$= \$ 85000 - \$ 60000 = \$ 25000 \text{ (use)}$$

Cash flow from investments = $ 15000 − $ 25000 = − $ 10000

(3) Financing cash flow.

Change in bond account = 2019 ending balance − 2018 ending balance

$$= \$ 15000 - \$ 10000 = \$ 5000 \ (\text{source})$$

$$\text{Change in common stock} = \$ 40000 - \$ 50000 = -\$ 10000 \ (\text{use})$$

$$\text{Cash dividends} = -\text{dividend} + \text{increase in dividends payable}$$

$$= -\$ 8500 + \$ 5000 = -\$ 3500 \ (\text{use})$$

$$\text{Cash flow from financing} = \$ 5000 - \$ 10000 - \$ 3500$$

$$= -\$ 8500$$

Note: if the dividend declared/paid amount is not provided, you can calculate the amount as follows: dividends declared = beginning retained earnings + net income − ending retained earnings.

Total cash flow:

Cash flow from operating	42500
Cash flow from investments	−10000
Cash flow from financing	−8500
Total cash flow:	$ 24000

If done correctly, the total cash flow will be equal to the increase in the cash balance over the period.

10.2.4 Interpretation of cash flows

Operating cash flow tells an analyst how much cash is being generated by the sales activity of the company. It is the most important component of cash flow analysis.

Negative operating cash flows indicate that the company will have to rely on external sources of financing to fund operations.

Interrelationships between cash flow components, such as cash inputs and cash collections, can give insight similar to ratio analysis with income statement figures.

Free cash flow (FCF) attempts to measure the cash available for discretionary purposes. This is the fundamental cash flow measure and is often used for valuation purposes. Formally, it should be the operating cash flow minus those cash flows necessary to maintain the firm's productive capacity and provide for growth. However, it is not practical for an analyst to determine which capital expenditures are necessary to maintain capacity and which are allotted for growth. Consequently, free cash flow is measured by:

Free cash flow = operating cash flow − net capital expenditures

$$= CFO - CFI$$

Where: Net capital expenditures = total capital expenditures − after-tax proceeds from asset sales

For valuation purposes, some adjustments to free cash flow must be made. If the analyst is interested in free cash flow to all investors, after-tax interest expense or $[I(1-t)]$ must be added back to CFO. If the analyst is interested in free cash flow to shareholders, debt repayments must be subtracted from CFO.

Example: Compute free cash flow for our sample company data in the previous example (assume a 35 percent tax rate)

Answer: Our best estimate of capital expenditures is the investing cash flows of the firm of− \$10000 (a cash outflow), hence:

$$\text{Free cash flow} = CFO - CFI$$
$$= \$42500 - \$10000$$
$$= \$32500$$

本章小结

一、本章要点与难点

（1）经营性现金流。

直接法：销售收入−生产投入−工资费用−利息费用−税收费用

间接法：净收益+折旧−记入损益表的投资性现金收入

（2）投资性现金流。

固定资产变量+固定资产处置盈利+证券投资变量

（3）融资性现金流。

融资资本变量−股利支付

二、Self-Test Problems

10-1　Using the following information in Table 10-3, what is the firm's cash flow from operations?

Table 10-3 Data to Calculate CFO ($)

Net income	120
Decrease in accounts receivable	20
Depreciation	25
Increase in inventory	10
Increase in accounts payable	7
Decrease in wages payable	5
Increase in deferred taxes	15
Profit from the sale of fixed assets	2

10-2   Using the following information in Table 10-4 to calculate CFO, CFI and CFF.

Table 10-4 Data to Calculate CFO, CFI and CFF ($)

Net income	45
Depreciation	75
Taxes paid	25
Interest paid	5
Dividends paid	10
Cash received from sale of company building	40
Sale of preferred stock	35
Repurchase of common stock	30
Purchase of machinery	20
Issuance of bonds	50
Debt retired through issuance of common stock	45
Paid off long-term bank borrowings	15
Profit on sale of building	20

Chapter 11
Dilutive Securities and EPS
（稀释证券及稀释每股收益）

Earnings per share（EPS）is one of the most commonly used corporate profitability performance measures for publicly traded firms.

Before calculating EPS you need to understand the following terms：

Dilutive（稀释性的）securities are stock options，warrants，convertible debt，or convertible preferred stock that would decrease EPS if exercised or converted to common stock.

Anti-dilutive（抗稀释）securities are securities that would increase EPS if exercised or converted to common stock.

All firms with complex capital structures[1] must report both basic and diluted EPS. Firms with simple capital structures [2]report only basic EPS.

The basic EPS calculation does not consider the effects of any dilutive securities in the computation of EPS.

$$\text{Basic EPS} = \frac{\text{net income} - \text{preferred dividends}}{\text{weighted average number of common shares outstanding}} \quad (11-1)$$

The current year's preferred dividends are subtracted from net income because EPS refers to the per-share earnings available to common shareholders.

Net income minus preferred dividends is the income available to common stockholders. Common stock dividends are not subtracted from net income because they are a part of the net income available to common shareholders.

---

[1] A complex capital structure contains potentially dilute securities such as options，warrants，or convertible securities.

[2] A simple capital structure is one that contains no potentially dilute securities. A simple capital structure contains only common stock，nonconvertible debt，and preferred stock.

The weighted average number of common shares is the number of shares outstanding during the year weighted by the portion of the year they were outstanding.

In computing weighted average number of shares, stock dividends[①] and stock splits[②] are considered to be changes in the number of common shares outstanding, not changes in the ownership of earnings. Stock dividends and splits do not change an owner's proportionate claim on the firm's earnings.

So, a stock split or dividend is applied to all shares issued prior to the split and to the beginning of period weighted average shares. The split or dividend is not applied to any shares that are issued or repurchased after the dividend or split date. In other words, the effect of stock dividends and splits is applied retroactively to the beginning of the year or the stock's issue date and is not weighted by the portion of the year after the stock dividend or split occurred.

Example: During 2018, Somy Inc. had net income of $100000, and it paid dividends of $50000 to its preferred stockholders, and paid $30000 in dividends to its common shareholders. Somy's common stock account are shown in the following Table 11-1:

Table 11-1 Somy's Common Stock Account

2018/01/01	Shares issued and outstanding at the beginning of the year	10000
2018/04/01	Shares issued	4000
2018/07/01	10% stock dividend	
2018/09/01	Shares repurchased for the treasury	3000

Compute the weighted average number of common shares outstanding during 2018, and compute EPS.

Answer:

———————————

① A stock dividend is the distribution of additional shares to each shareholder in an amount proportional to their current number of shares. If a 10 percent stock dividend is paid, the holder of 100 shares of stock would receive 10 additional shares.

② A stock split refers to the division of each "old" share into a specific number of "new" (post split) shares. The holder of 100 shares will have 200 shares after a 2-for-1 split or 150 shares after a 3-for-2 split.

Step 1: adjust the number of pre-dividend shares to their post dividend units to reflect the 10 percent stock dividend by multiplying all share numbers prior to the stock dividend by 1. 1 (see Table 11-2). Shares issued or retired after the stock dividend are not affected.

Table 11-2   Adjustment

2018/01/01	Initial shares issued adjusted for the 10% dividend	11000
2018/04/01	Shares issued adjusted for the 10% dividend	4400
2018/09/01	Shares repurchased for the treasury (no adjustment)	-3000

Step 2: compute the weighted average number of post-stock dividend shares[1] (see Table 11-3).

Table 11-3   Weighted Average Number

Initial shares	(11000) (12 months outstanding)	132000
Issued shares	(4400) (9 months outstanding)	39600
Retired treasury shares	(-3000) (4 months retired)[2]	-12000
Total share-month		159600
Average shares	159600/12	13300

Step 3: compute basic EPS.

$$\text{Basic EPS} = \frac{\text{net income-preferred dividend}}{\text{weighted average shares of common stock}}$$

$$= \frac{\$100000 - \$50000}{13300} = \$3.76^{[3]}$$

With a simple capital structure, only basic EPS is reported. If a firm has a complex capital structure containing dilutive securities (convertibles and options), then in com-

---

① The weighting system is days outstanding divided by the number of days in a year. Shares issued enter into the computation from the date of issuance. But for simple, the monthly approximation method will probably be used.

② Reacquired shares are excluded from the computation from the date of reacquisition.

③ Previously reported EPS data is restated to reflect stock splits and dividends.

puting diluted EPS we will treat these securities as if they were converted to common stock from the first of the year. Basic EPS does not consider dilutive securities in its computation. Neither basic nor diluted EPS calculations consider anti-dilutive securities.

The numerator of the basic EPS equation contains income available to common shareholders (net income minus preferred dividends). In the case of diluted EPS, if there are dilutive securities (e. g. convertible preferred stock, convertible bonds, or warrants) that will cause the weighted average common shares to change, then the numerator must be adjusted as the following:

If convertible preferred stock is dilutive (meaning EPS will decrease if the stock is converted), the convertible preferred dividends must be added back to the previously calculated income from continuing operations minus preferred dividends.

If convertible bonds are dilutive, then the bonds' after-tax interest expense would not be considered as an interest expense for diluted EPS. Hence, interest expense multiplied by $(1-t)$ must be added back to the numerator.

The denominator contains the number of shares of common stock issued, weighted by the days that the shares have been outstanding. When considering dilutive securities, the denominator is the basic EPS denominator adjusted for the equivalent number of common shares created by the conversion of all outstanding dilutive securities (convertible bonds, convertible preferred shares, warrants, and options).

Stock options and warrants are dilutive only when their exercise price is less than the average market price of the stock over the year. Dilutive stock options and/or warrants increase the number of common shares outstanding in the denominator for diluted EPS. There is no adjustment to net income in the numerator. If there are restrictions on the proceeds received when warrants are exercised (e. g. must be used to retire debt), then diluted EPS calculations must reflect the results of those agreements.

Use the treasury stock method to calculate the adjustment to the number of shares in the denominator when there're dilutive stock options or warrants. .

The treasury stock method assumes that the hypothetical funds received by the company from the exercise of the options are used to purchase shares of the company's common stock in the market at the average market price.

The treasury stock method reduces the total increase in shares created from the hypothetical exercise of the options into common stock.

The net increase in the number of shares outstanding (the adjustment to the denominator) will be the number of shares created by exercising the options minus the number of shares repurchased with the proceeds of exercise.

The diluted EPS equation (assuming convertible securities are dilutive) is:

$$\text{Diluted EPS} = \frac{\text{adjusted income available for common shares}}{\text{weighted average common and potential common shares outstanding}} \tag{11-2}$$

The adjusted income available for common shares is:

Net income−Preferred dividends+Dividends on convertible preferred stock+After−tax interest on convertible debt

Adjusted income available for common shares

Therefore, diluted EPS is:

$$\text{Diluted EPS} = \frac{\begin{bmatrix} \text{net} & -\text{preferred} \\ \text{income} & \text{dividends} \end{bmatrix} + \begin{bmatrix} \text{convertible} \\ \text{preferred} \\ \text{dividends} \end{bmatrix} + \begin{bmatrix} \text{convertible} \\ \text{debt} \\ \text{interest} \end{bmatrix} (1-t)}{\begin{bmatrix} \text{weighted} \\ \text{average} \\ \text{shares} \end{bmatrix} + \begin{bmatrix} \text{shares from conversion of} \\ \text{convertible preferred shares} \end{bmatrix} + \begin{bmatrix} \text{shares from} \\ \text{conversion of} \\ \text{convertible debt} \end{bmatrix} + \begin{bmatrix} \text{shares} \\ \text{issuable from} \\ \text{stock options} \end{bmatrix}} \tag{11-3}$$

Remember, each potentially dilutive security must be examined separately to determine if it is actually dilutoive (EPS would be reduced if converted to common stock).

Example: During 2018, Somy Inc. reported net income of $115600 and had 200000 shares of common stock outstanding for the entire year. Somy also had 1000 shares of 10 percent, $100 par preferred stock outstanding during 2003. During 2002, Somy issued 600, $1000 par, 7 percent bonds for $600000 (issued at par). Each of these bonds is convertible to 100 shares of common stock. The tax rate is 40 percent. Compute the basic and diluted EPS in 2018.

Answer:

Step 1: compute basic EPS.

$$\text{Basic EPS} = \frac{\$\,115600 - \$\,10000}{200000} = \$\,0.53$$

Step 2: calculate diluted EPS.

Compute the increase in common stock outstanding if the convertible debt is converted to common stock at the beginning of 2018:

Shares issuable for debt conversion = 600×100 = 60000 shares

If the convertible debt is converted to common stock at the beginning of 2018, then there would be no interest expense related to the convertible debt. Therefore, it is necessary to increase Somy's after-tax net income for the after-tax effect of the decrease in interest expense:

Increase in income = [(600) (\$1000) (0.07)] (1 − 0.40) = \$25200

Compute diluted EPS as if the convertible debt were common stock:

$$\text{Diluted EPS} = \frac{\text{net income} - \text{preferred dividends} + \text{covertible debt interest}(1-t)}{\text{weighted average shares} + \text{convertible debt shares}}$$

$$= \frac{\$\,115600 - \$\,10000 + \$\,25200}{200000 + 60000} = \$\,0.50$$

Check to make sure that diluted EPS is less than basic EPS [\$0.50 < \$0.53]. If diluted EPS is more than the basic EPS, the convertible bonds are anti-dilutive and should not be treated as common stock in computing diluted EPS.

A quick way to determine whether the convertible debt is dilutive is to calculate its per share impact by:

$$\frac{\text{convertible debt interest}(1-t)}{\text{convertible debt shares}} \qquad (11-4)$$

If this per share amount is grater than basic EPS, the convertible debt is anti-dilutive and should be excluded from the calculation of diluted EPS.

If this per share amount is less than basic EPS, the convertible debt is dilutive and should be included in the calculation of diluted EPS.

Example: During 2018, Somy reported net income of \$115600 and had 200000 shares of common stock and 1000 shares of preferred stock outstanding for the entire year. Each of Somy's 10 percent, \$100 par value preferred-stock share is convertible into 40 shares of common stock. The tax rate is 40 percent. Compute the basic and diluted EPS in 2018.

Answer:

Step 1: calculate basic EPS.

$$\text{Basic EPS} = \frac{\$115600 - \$10000}{200000} = \$0.53$$

Step 2: calculate diluted EPS.

Compute the increase in common stock outstanding if the preferred stock is converted to common stock at the beginning of 2018: $1000 \times 40 = 40000$ shares.

If the convertible preferred stock were converted to common stock, there would be no preferred dividends paid. Therefore, you should add back the convertible preferred dividends that had previously been subtracted.

Compute diluted EPS as if the convertible preferred stock were common stock:

$$\text{Diluted EPS} = \frac{\text{net income} - \text{preferred dividends} + \text{convertible debt interest}(1-t)}{\text{weighted average shares} + \text{convertible preferred common shares}}$$

$$= \frac{\$115600 - \$10000 + \$10000}{200000 + 40000} = \$0.48$$

Check to make sure that diluted EPS is less than basic EPS. [$0.48 < $0.53]. If diluted EPS is more than the basic EPS, the preferred stock are anti-dilutive and should not be treated as common stock in computing diluted EPS.

Example: During 2018, Somy reported net income of $115600 and had 200000 shares of common stock outstanding for the entire year. Somy also had 1000 shares of 10 percent, par $100 preferred stock outstanding during 2018. Somy has 10000 stock options outstanding the entire year. Each option allows its holder to purchase 1 share of common stock at $15 per share. The average market price of Somy's common stock during 2018 is $20 per share. Compute the diluted EPS.

Answer: Number of common shares created if the options are exercised: 10000 shares
Cash inflow if the options are exercised ($15/share)(10000) = $150000
Number of shares that can be purchased with these funds is: $150000/

$\$20 = 7500$ shares

Net increase in common shares outstanding from the exercise of the stock options：2500 shares

$$\text{Diluted EPS} = \frac{\$115600 - 1000 \times 10\% \times \$100}{200000 + 2500} = \frac{\$115600 - \$10000}{200000 + 2500} = \$0.52$$

本章小结

一、本章要点与难点

（1）基本每股净收益：

$$\text{Basic EPS} = \frac{\text{net income} - \text{preferred dividends}}{\text{weighted average number of common shares outstanding}}$$

（2）具有稀释可能性的证券。

可转换债券：$\text{EPS} = \dfrac{\begin{bmatrix} \text{net} & -\text{preferred} \\ \text{income} & \text{dividends} \end{bmatrix} + \begin{bmatrix} \text{convertible} \\ \text{debt} \\ \text{interest} \end{bmatrix}(1-t)}{\begin{bmatrix} \text{weighted} \\ \text{average} \\ \text{shares} \end{bmatrix} + \begin{bmatrix} \text{shares from} \\ \text{conversion of} \\ \text{convertible debt} \end{bmatrix}}$

当 EPS< Basic EPS 时，该可转换债券为稀释性证券。

可转换优先股：$\text{EPS} = \dfrac{\begin{bmatrix} \text{net} & -\text{preferred} \\ \text{income} & \text{dividends} \end{bmatrix} + \begin{bmatrix} \text{convertible} \\ \text{preferred} \\ \text{dividends} \end{bmatrix}}{\begin{bmatrix} \text{weighted} \\ \text{average} \\ \text{shares} \end{bmatrix} + \begin{bmatrix} \text{shares from} \\ \text{conversion of} \\ \text{convertible preferred shares} \end{bmatrix}}$

当 EPS< Basic EPS 时，该可转换优先股为稀释性证券。

股票期权：EPS =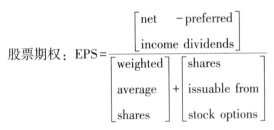

当 EPS< Basic EPS 时，该股票期权为稀释性证券。

（3）稀释的每股收益：

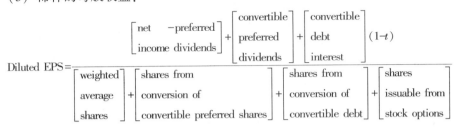

二、Self-Test Problems

11-1 During 2018, Titic Inc. had net income of ＄100000, and paid dividends of ＄50000 to its preferred stockholders, and paid ＄30000 in dividends to its common shareholders. Titic's common stock account are shown in the following Table 11-4：

Table 11-4 Titic's Common Stock Account

2018/01/01	Shares issued and outstanding at the beginning of the year	20000
2018/04/01	Shares issued	5000
2018/07/01	10% stock dividend	
2018/08/01	Stock split 3-for-2	
2018/11/01	Shares repurchased for the treasury	6000

Compute the weighted average number of common shares outstanding during 2018, and compute EPS.

11-2 Robu Inc. reported ＄100000 of net income for 2018 on weighted average common shares outstanding of 12500. Robu had ＄400000 face value of convertible bonds outstanding with an annual coupon rate of 6 percent. The bonds were issued on April 12018 and can be converted into common shares at a conversion ratio of 20 shares with a ＄1000 face value per share. Robu also had 5000 outstanding warrants with an exercise price of ＄40 that were issued on December 312017. The average share price during the year was ＄45, and the marginal tax rate is 35 percent. Calculate basic and diluted EPS.

11-3　Park Services Inc. reported ＄100000 of net income for 2017 on weighted average common shares outstanding of 12500. Park has ＄400000 face value of convertible bonds outstanding with an annual coupon rate of 15 percent. The bonds were issued on April 12017 and can be converted into common shares at a conversion ratio of 10 shares with a ＄1000 face value per share. Park also had 5000 outstanding warrants with an exercise price of ＄40 that were issued on December 312016. The average share price during the year was ＄45, and the marginal tax rate is 35 percent. Calculate basic and diluted EPS.

Chapter 12
Analysis of Inventories
（存货分析）

The choice of accounting method used to account for inventory affects the firm's income statement, balance sheet, related financial ratios, and more importantly, the cash flows.

To begin with, try to remember and understand a basic inventory formula which relates the beginning balance, purchases, and cost of goods sold (COGS) to the ending balance.

$$\text{Ending inventory} = \text{beginning inventory} + \text{purchases} - \text{COGS} \qquad (12-1)$$

This equation is rearranged for several purposes, such as:

$$\text{Purchases} = \text{ending inventory} - \text{beginning inventory} + \text{COGS} \qquad (12-2)$$

or

$$\text{COGS} = \text{purchases} + \text{beginning inventory} - \text{ending inventory} \qquad (12-3)$$

Now, let's use the following data to introduce three methods of inventory accounting. Consider the following inventory data in Table 12-1:

Table 12-1　Inventory Data （$）

January 1 (beginning inventory)	2 units at $2 per unit	4
January 7 purchase	3 units at $3 per unit	9
January 19 purchase	5 units at $5 per unit	25
Cost of goods available	10 units	38
Units sold during January	7 units	—

12. 1　First in, First out (FIFO，先进先出)

The cost of inventory first acquired (beginning inventory and early purchases) is assigned to the cost of goods sold for the period.

The cost of the most recent purchases is assigned to ending inventory (see Table 12-2).

Table 12-2　FIFO COGS Calculation ($)

From beginning inventory	2 units at $ 2 per unit	4
From first purchase	3 units at $ 3 per unit	9
From second purchase	2 units at $ 5 per unit	10
FIFO cost of goods sold	7 units	23
Ending inventory	3 units at $ 5 per unit	15

12. 2　Last in, First out (LIFO，后进先出)

The cost of inventory most recently purchased is assigned to the cost of goods sold for the period.

The cost of beginning inventory and earlier purchases go to ending inventory (see Table 12-3).

Table 12-3　LIFO COGS Calculation ($)

From second purchase	5 units at $ 5 per unit	25
From first purchase	2 units at $ 3 per unit	6
LIFO cost of goods sold	7 units	31
Ending inventory	2 units at $ 2 per unit and 1 unit at $ 3	7

12.3　Average Cost

Average cost calculates cost per unit by dividing cost of goods available by total u-nits available. This average cost is used to determine both cost of goods sold and ending inventory (see Table 12-4).

Table 12-4　Weighted Average COGS Calculation（$）

Average unit cost	38/10	3. 8 per unit
Weighted average cost of goods sold	7 units at $3. 8 per unit	26. 60
Ending inventory	3 units at $3. 8 per unit	11. 40

From the above tables, we could see during periods of rising prices, LIFO cost of goods sold is greater than FIFO cost of goods sold. Therefore, LIFO net income will be less than FIFO net income. And LIFO inventory is also less than FIFO inventory (see Table 12-5). This results in LIFO profitability ratios being smaller than ratios under FIFO.

If financial statements are analyzed and compared with firms using different cost flow assumptions, then adjustments have to be made to achieve comparability.

Table 12-5　LIFO and FIFO Comparison (Rising Prices and Stable or Increasing Inventories)

LIFO results in	FIFO results in
Higher COGS	Lower COGS
Lower taxes	Higher taxes
Lower net income (EBT and EAT)	Higher net income (EBT and EAT)
Lower inventory balances	Higher inventory balances
Lower working capital	Higher working capital
Higher cash flows (less taxes paid out)	Lower cash flows (more taxes paid out)

Oftentimes, an analyst wants to compare a company to other companies in the same industry. When two companies use different methods of accounting for inventory, one of the firm's inventories must be adjusted in order to make the comparison relevant. There are two types of conversion: LIFO to FIFO and FIFO to LIFO.

12.4   From LIFO to FIFO

The LIFO to FIFO conversion is relatively simple because companies that use LIFO also report a LIFO reserve[1]—The difference between what their ending inventory would have been under FIFO accounting and its value under LIFO.

$$\text{LIFO reserve} = Inv_F - Inv_L \qquad (12-4)$$

Where:

Int_F = inventory value under FIFO

Int_L = inventory value under LIFO

To convert LIFO inventory balances to a FIFO basis, we can simply add the LIFO reserve to the LIFO inventory:

$$Int_F = Int_L + \text{LIFO reserve} \qquad (12-5)$$

The conversion from LIFO COGS to FIFO is slightly more complicated. Now, we begin with the basic inventory accounting equation of (12-1):

$$\text{Ending inventory} = \text{beginning inventory} + \text{purchases} - \text{COGS}$$

For FIFO, we have:

$$EI_F = BI_F + \text{purchases} - COGS_F \qquad (12-6)$$

For LIFO, we have:

$$EI_L = BI_L + \text{purchases} - COGS_L \qquad (12-7)$$

Where:

EI_F = the ending inventory level under FIFO

EI_L = the ending inventory level under LIFO

BI_F = the beginning inventory value under FIFO

BI_L = the beginning inventory value under LIFO

---

[1]   The LIFO reserve is typically shown in the footnotes to the financial statements.

$COGS_F$ = the COGS under FIFO

$COGS_L$ = the COGS under LIFO

Let's use equation (12−6) minus equation (12−7), that is:

$$EI_F - EI_L = (BI_F - BI_L) - COGS_F + COGS_L \qquad (12-8)$$

From the concept of LIFO reserve we find that $(EI_F - EI_L)$ is the reserve at the end of the period (LIFO reserve$_E$), and $(BI_F - BI_L)$ is the reserve at the beginning of the period (LIFO reserve$_B$), so we rewrite the equation (12−8):

$$COGS_F = COGS_L - (\text{LIFO reserve}_E - \text{LIFO reserve}_B) \qquad (12-9)$$

It's really a long way. While the quick way to convert COGS from LIFO to FIFO is to use the formula directly:

$$COGS_F = COGS_L - \text{change in the LIFO reserve}$$
$$= COGS_L - (\text{LIFO reserve}_E - \text{LIFO reserve}_B)$$

Where:

$COGS_F$ = the COGS under FIFO

$COGS_L$ = the COGS under LIFO

LIFO reserve$_E$ = the reserve at the end of the period

LIFO reserve$_B$ = the reserve at the beginning of the period

Example: Converting from LIFO to FIFO

Somy Inc. which uses LIFO, reported end of year inventory balances of $500 in 2002 and $700 in 2003. The LIFO reserve was $200 for 2002 and $300 for 2003. COGS during 2003 was $3000. Convert 2003 ending inventory and COGS to a FIFO basis.

Answer:

Inventory:

$$Int_F = Int_L + \text{LIFO reserve}$$
$$= \$700 + \$300$$
$$= \$1000$$

COGS:

$$COGS_F = COGS_L - \text{change in the LIFO reserve}$$
$$= COGS_L - (\text{LIFO reserve}_E - \text{LIFO reserve}_B)$$
$$= \$3000 - (\$300 - \$200)$$
$$= \$2900$$

12.5   From FIFO to LIFO

FIFO to LIFO conversions are typically not done for inventory, since inventory under LIFO is not a reflection of true economic value. However, it may be useful to consider what COGS would be under LIFO. The adjustment process is completely different with the process of converting COGS from LIFO to FIFO. There is no precise calculation; an analyst must estimate what the costs would have been under LIFO.

The estimate of COGS is:

$$COGS_L = COGS_F + (BI_F \times \text{inflation rate}) \qquad (12-10)$$

The inflation rate should not be a general inflation rate for the economy but an inflation rate appropriate for that firm or industry.

The increase in the LIFO reserve for another company in the same industry divided by that company's beginning inventory level converted to FIFO accounting.

An analyst can also estimate what the COGS would have been under the LIFO method for a company that uses the average cost method, because the average cost method always reports inventory values and costs of goods sold between values reported under LIFO and FIFO, the adjustment for the COGS estimate should be half of the adjustment used for FIFO accounting:

$$COGS_L = COGS_W + 1/2(BI_W \times \text{inflation rate}) \qquad (12-11)$$

Where:

$COGS_W$ = the COGS under the average cost method

BI_W = the beginning inventory under the average cost method

Example: FIFO to LIFO conversion

ABC Inc. is in the same industry as Somy from the previous example. ABC uses FIFO accounting and has COGS of $2000, ending inventory of $500, and beginning inventory of $350. Estimate ABC's COGS under LIFO accounting.

Answer:

First estimate the inflation rate using data of Somy. The increase in the

LIFO reserve for Somy is ＄300－＄200＝＄100. The beginning inventory converted to FIFO is ＄700. That means the inflation rate is ＄100/ ＄700＝14.2%.

Now the estimate of COGS can be calculated as:

$$COGS_L = COGS_F + (BI_F \times \text{inflation rate})$$
$$= \$2000 + (\$350 \times 14.2\%)$$
$$= \$2050$$

Since the choice of inventory accounting method has an impact on income statement and balance sheet items, it will have an impact on ratios as well. In general, an analyst should use LIFO values when examining profitability or cost ratios and FIFO values when examining asset or equity ratios.

本章小结

一、本章要点与难点

（1）从 LIFO 转换成 FIFO。

存货价值：$Int_F = Int_L + \text{LIFO reserve}$

已售成本：$COGS_F = COGS_L - (\text{LIFO reserve}_E - \text{LIFO reserve}_B)$

（2）从 FIFO 转换成 LIFO。

已售成本：$COGS_L = COGS_F + (BI_F \times \text{inflation rate})$

二、Self-Test Problems

12-1　Kerka Inc. sells bowling balls. The following information is relevant for the year ended December 31, 2017.

purchases	sales
40 units at ＄30	13 units at ＄35
20 units at ＄40	35 units at ＄45
90 units at ＄50	60 units at ＄60

Assume that beginning inventory consists of 20 units at ＄25 and tax rate is 40 percent.

a. What is the year-end inventory balance under FIFO?

b. What is the gross profit for the year end under LIFO?

c. What is the year-end LIFO reserve?

12-2　The beginning of period LIFO reserve is ＄50000, and the end of period LIFO reserve is ＄60000. What are the financial statement adjustments if the firm's tax rate is 40 percent.

a. To adjust endof period LIFO inventory to FIFO inventory.

b. To adjust end of period retained earnings from LIFO based to FIFO based inventory accounting.

c. To adjust COGS from LIFO to FIFO, you must adjust the LIFO COGS by?

Chapter 13
Analysis of Multinational Operations
(跨国经营分析)

The issue addressed is how to reflect the results of foreign operating units in the consolidated financial statements of the multinational parent company. The following are some necessary concepts you should be armed with.

13. 1　Flow and Holding Effects

Exchange rates can impact the reporting of the firm's financial statements in two ways: ①flow effects and ②holding gain/loss effects. **Flow effects** are the impact of changes in the exchange rate on income statement items such as revenue. **Holding gain/loss effects** are the impact of changes in the exchange rate on assets and liabilities on the balance sheet, such as cash balances. The best way to illustrate these effects is with an example.

Example: A U. S. firm owns a subsidiary located in a foreign country with a local currency (LC). In 2018 the subsidiary generated revenue of LC2000. In 2019, revenue increased by 20 percent to LC2400. The average exchange rates in 2018 and 2019 were, respectively, LC = $ 1. 00 and LC = $ 1. 20. Determine which portion of the dollar increase in revenue is attribu table to the flow effect (the effect of the change in the exchange rate) and which portion is due to the 20 percent revenue growth of the subsidiary.

Answer: As is shown in Table 13–1.

Table 13-1   Illustration of the Flow Effect

	2018	2019	Total	Change in LC or $
Exchange rate	LC = $ 1. 00	LC = $ 1. 20		
Revenues (LC)	LC2000	LC2400	LC4400	LC400
Revenues ($)	$ 2000	$ 2880	$ 4880	$ 880
Flow effect				$ 480

The $ 880 increase in revenue is attribuTable to two components.

One is the $ 400 (LC400× $ 1. 00/LC) increase in local currency revenue. In other words, revenue from the subsidiary would have increased by $ 400 if the exchange rate had not changed.

The other is the flow effect of $ 480 (LC2400× $ 0. 2 change in the exchange rate).

Example：Let's continue with the previous example and assume that the subsidiary keeps all of the revenue on its balance sheet as cash. Calculate the cash balance in dollars on the consolidated balance sheet at the end of 2018 and 2019. Determine the holding gain/loss effect on the cash balance resulting from the change in the exchange rate.

Answer：As is shown in Table 13-2.

Table 13-2   Illustration of the Holding Effect

	2018	2019
Exchange rate	LC = $ 1. 00	LC = $ 1. 20
Cash (LC)	LC2000	LC4400
Cash ($)	$ 2000	$ 5280

There two ways to calculate the holding gain/loss effect：

Total revenue in dollars was $ 4880 (from Table 13-1), but the cumulative cash balance at the end of 2019 was $ 5280, so the holding effect was a gain of $ 400, that is $ 5280- $ 4880.

The LC2000 in cash on the balance sheet at the end of 2019 increased in value by $400, that is LC2000× ($1.20/LC – $1.00/LC) at the end of 2019.

Let's summarize the analysis. If the exchange rate had remained constant at LC = $1.00, the parent company would have reported cash on the consolidated balance sheet from the subsidiary at the end of 2019 of $4400, that is (LC4400 × $1.00/LC); the actual amount was $5280. This $880's gain is attributable to:

Flow effect of $480 (LC2400× $0.2/LC).

Holding gain effect of $400 (LC2000× $0.2/LC).

13.1.1 Currency Definitions

The **local currency** (东道国货币) is the currency of the country in which the foreign subsidiary is located.

The **functional currency** (记账本位币) is defined as the currency of the primary economic environment in which the foreign subsidiary generates and expends cash. The choice reflects management's judgment. It can be the currency in which the subsidiary conducts operations or some other currency.

The **reporting currency** (报告货币) is the currency in which the multinational firm prepares its final, consolidated financial statements.

13.1.2 Other Definitions

The following definitions are also necessary to understand accounting for multinational operations and will be used in subsequent sections.

The **current rate** is the exchange rate as of the balance sheet date.

The **average rate** is the average exchange rate over the reporting period.

The **historical rate** is the rate that exists when a particular transaction is conducted.

Re-measurement is the translation of local currency transactions into the functional currency.

Translation is the conversion of the functional currency of a subsidiary into the reporting currency.

13. 2　All-Current Method vs.　Temporal Method

Note that re-measurement is the process of converting the local currency into the functional currency using the temporal method, with gains and losses flowing to the income statement. The all-current method, or translation, is the process of converting the functional currency into the reporting currency, with gains and loses flowing to the balance sheet as an adjustment to equity.

13. 2. 1　Temporal Method

The provisions of the temporal method state that:

Cash, accounts receivable, accounts payable, short-term debt, and long-term debt (defined as monetary assets and liabilities) are translated using the current rate.

All other assets and liabilities (Non-monetary assets and liabilities) are translated at the historical rate. Hence, a major drawback of the temporal method is that you need to keep track of many different historical exchange rates. (Non-monetary items you're likely to encounter are inventory and fixed assets)

Revenues and expenses are translated at the average rate.

Purchases of inventory and fixed assets ate re-measured at the historical rate as of the date of purchase. Therefore, re-measurement of cost of goods sold and depreciation is based on historical rates prevailing at the time of purchase.

The translation gain or loss is shown onthe income statement. This is seen as another major drawback to the temporal method, because exchange rate volatility is reflected in the net income of the firm. This forces managers to decide between hedging the economic effects and the accounting effects of foreign exchange volatility.

Example: Translating inventory and COGS under the temporal method

　　Table 13-3 contains information and calculation related to the purchases and sales of a foreign subsidiary of a U. S. corporation. For simplicity, we assume that each unit purchased costs 1 Local Currency (LC). At the beginning of 2018, the rate is LC = \$ 1. 00. Inventory was acquired at LC1. 10= \$ 1. 00 and LC0. 95= \$ 1. 00 in 2018 and 2019, respectively.

The calculations for COGS and ending inventory balances in LC are straightforward using the inventory accounting relationship:

COGS=beginning inventory+purchases−ending inventory

Under FIFO, we assume that the units in inventory at the beginning of the year are sold off during the year and that the ending balance consists of units purchased during the year. Under FIFO these units are valued at the exchange rate the purchases were made. Under LIFO, the units sold during the year are the ones purchased during the year, and the ending inventory balance is valued at the historical rate.

Table 13-3   FIFO/LIFO and Exchange Rate Effects

		LC	FIFO		LIFO	
			Rate	\$	Rate	\$
2018	Beginning balance	200	1. 00	200①	1. 00	200
	Purchases	250	1. 10	227②	1. 10	227
	Units sold	300				
	Ending balance	150	1. 10	136	1. 00	150
	COGS	300		291		277
2019	Beginning balance	150	1. 10	136	1. 00	150
	Purchases	250	0. 95	263	0. 95	263
	Units sold	300				
	Ending balance	100	0. 95	105	1. 00	100
	COGS	300		294		313

① $\frac{LC200}{1.00LC/\$} = \$200.$

② $\frac{LC250}{1.10LC/\$} = \$227.$

Table 13-4 provides some general intuition on the compound effects of changing exchange rates and the choice of FIFO versus LIFO accounting methods on the translated COGS and ending inventory measures.

Table 13-4 Translated COGS and Ending Inventory under FIFO and LIFO

	FIFO	LIFO
Depreciating local currency（2018）	Higher COGS Lower ending inventory	Lower COGS Higher ending inventory
Appreciating local currency（2019）	Lower COGS Higher ending inventory	Higher COGS Lower ending inventory

13. 2. 2 All-Current Method

The all-current method is much easier to apply than the temporal method because:

All income statement accounts are translated at the average rate.

All balance sheet accounts are translated at the current rate except common stock, which is translated at the appropriate historical rate that applied when the equity was issued.

Dividends are translated at the rate that applied when they were paid.

The cumulative translation adjustment is included on the balance sheet as part of equity.

13. 2. 3 Choice of Appropriate Method

Now we can turn our attention to the issue of which translation method is appropriate to use for a given set of circumstances. The first step in determining which method should be used is to identify the functional currency. This choice determines whether the temporal method or the current rate method will be used.

The following rules govern the determination of the functional currency:

（1）the results of operations, financial position, and cash flows of all foreign operations must be measured in the designated functional currency.

（2）Treatment of subsidiaries: Self-contained, independent subsidiaries whose operating, investing, and financing activities are primarily located in the local market will use the local currency as the functional currency.

Subsidiaries whose operations are well integrated with the parent (the parent makes the operating, financing, and investing decisions) will use the parent's currency as the functional currency.

Subsidiaries that operate in highly inflationary environments will use the parent's currency as the functional currency. A high inflation environment is defined as cumulative inflation that exceeds 100 percent over a three-year period.

If the functional currency is the local currency, use the all-current method, the use of the all-current method is called translation

If the functional currency is the parent's currency or some other currency, use the temporal method. The use of the temporal method is called re-measurement.

Finally, a third currency may serve as the functional currency when a subsidiary is operating relatively independently in a market where the local currency, prices, and some costs are controlled or restricted. For example, if a subsidiary of the U. S. parent is operating is China, the Hong Kong dollar might be the functional currency.

Figure 13-1 illustrates the three ways a local currency may be re-measured and/ or translated into the reporting currency for the parent. Note the choice of the functional currency determines the methods used for conversion.

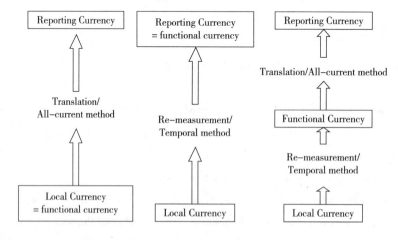

Figure 13-1 Three Methods for Re-measurement/Translation of Local Currencies

Example: A U. S. multinational firm has a Japanese subsidiary. It has determined
that the Japanese yen is the functional currency. Determine which
foreign currency translation method is appropriate.

Answer: In this case, translation is needed, since the local currency is the functional currency. Use the all-current method to translate the subsidiary's
data to U. S. dollars.

13. 3   Translation Gains/Losses Calculation

Table 13-5 summarizes the exchange rate used to translate the results of foreign
subsidiaries under the temporal method and the all-current method.

Table 13-5   Exchange Rate Usage under the Temporal and All-current Method

Account	Rate used to translate account using the two methods	
	Temporal method	All-current method
Monetary assets and liabilities	Current rate	Current rate
Non-monetary assets/liabilities	Historical rate	Current rate
Common stock and dividends	Historical rate	Historical rate
Equity (taken as a whole)	Blended rate	Current rate
Revenues and SG&A	Average rate	Average rate
Cost of goods sold	Historical rate	Average rate
Depreciation	Historical rate	Average rate
Net income	Blended rate	Average rate

Translation gains or losses result from gains or losses related to balance sheet accounts that are translated at the current rate.

We can use this insight to calculate the translation gain or loss under either the all-
current or the temporal method by first calculating the net exposure under each method,
and then calculating the flow effect and the holding gain/loss effect associated with that

exposure.

Under the all-current method, all assets and liabilities are translated at the current rate, so the net exposure is assets minus liabilities, or total shareholders' equity:

Exposure under the all-current method = total shareholders' equity + liabilities

Under the temporal method, only cash, accounts receivable, accounts payable, current debt, and long-term debt are translated at the current rate:

Exposure under the temporal method =

(cash+accounts receivable) − (accounts payable+current debt+long-term debt)

The flow effect measured in u. s. dollars under both methods is equal to the change in exposure times the difference between the ending rate and the average rate:

Flow effects (in $) = change in exposure (in LC)×(ending rate−average rate)

The holding gain/loss effect measured in $ is the beginning exposure times the difference between the exchange rate at the end of the year and the exchange rate at the beginning of the year:

Holding gain/loss effect (in $)= beginning exposure (in LC) ×

(ending rate−beginning rate)

The total translation gain or loss measured in $ is the sum of the two effects:

Translation gain/loss (in $)= flow effect+holding gain/loss effect

Under the all-current method, the translation gains/losses are accumulated on the balance sheet in the equity section as part of comprehensive income in an account called the cumulative translation adjustment (CTA).

Under the temporal method, the translation gain/loss appears on the income statement.

Example: The all-current method

Somy international is a U. S. company with a subsidiary named Doby Inc. located in the country of ABC. Doby was acquired by Somy on 12/31/2018. Somy reports its financial results in U. S. dollars. The currency of ABC is loca (LC). Doby's financial statements of 2019 are shown in Table 13−6 and Table 13−7.

The following exchange rates between U. S. dollar and loca were observed:

December 31, 2018: LC2.00 = \$1.00; \$0.50 = LC1.00

December 31, 2019: LC2.20 = \$1.00; \$0.4545 = LC1.00

Average for 2019: LC2.10 = \$1.00; \$0.4672 = LC1.00

Historical rate for fixed assets, inventory, and equity: LC2.00 = \$1.00; \$0.50 = LC1.00

The majority of Doby's operational, financial, and investment decisions are made at Doby's headquarter in ABC. Use the appropriate method to translate Doby's 2019 balance sheet and income statement into U.S. dollars.

Answer: Doby is relatively self-contained, which means loca is the functional currency and the appropriate method is the all-current method. The all-current method uses the current rate for all balance sheet accounts (except common stock, which is translated at the historical rate) and the average rate for all income statement accounts. The translation gain or loss appears is the CTA in the equity section as part of comprehensive income.

Let's first calculate the translation gain/loss for 2019.

Ending exposure = LC1200

Beginning exposure = LC500

Change in exposure = LC1200 − LC500 = LC700

Flow effect = LC700 × (0.4545 − 0.4762) = − \$15.2

Holding loss effect = LC500 × (0.4545 − 0.50) = − \$22.7

Translation loss for 2008 = − \$15.2 − \$22.7 = − \$37.9

The cumulative translation adjustment for 2019 equals the beginning balance of zero (Because Doby was acquired at the end of 2018, the CTA attribuTable to Doby was zero on that date) plus the translation loss for the year: \$0 + (− \$37.9) = − \$37.9.

Doby's translated 2019 income statement is shown in Table 13−8. Notice that we translate the income statement first with the all−current method to derive net income, which we then use to calculate retained earnings on the balance sheet.

Table 13-6 Doby's Balance Sheet on December 31, 2018 and 2019 (in LC)

	2018	2019
Cash	100	100
Accounts receivable	500	650
Inventory	1000	1200
Current assets	1600	1950
Fixed assets	800	1600
Accumulated depreciation	(100)	(700)
Net fixed assets	700	900
Total assets	2300	2850
Accounts payable	400	500
Current debt	100	200
Long-term debt	1300	950
Total liabilities	1800	1650
Common stock	400	400
Retained earnings	100	800
Total equity	500	1200
Total liabilities and shareholders' equity	2300	2850

Table 13-7 Doby's 2019 Income Statement (in LC)

	2019
Revenue	5000
Cost of goods sold	(3300)
Gross margin	1700
Other expenses	(400)
Depreciation expense	(600)
Net income	700

Table 13-8 Doby's 2019 Translated Income Statement under the All-current Method

	2019 (LC)	Rate ($ /LC)	2019 ($)
Revenue	5000	0. 4762	2381. 0
Cost of goods sold	(3300)	0. 4762	(1571. 5)
Gross margin	1700		809. 5
Other expenses	(400)	0. 4762	(190. 5)
Depreciation expense	(600)	0. 4762	(285. 7)
Net income	700		333. 3

Beginning (2018) retained earnings in U. S. dollars was $LC100 \times \$ 0. 50/LC = \$ 50$, so ending (2019) retained earnings are $\$ 50 + \$ 333. 3 = \$ 383. 3$.

Doby's 2019 translated balance sheet is shown in Table 13-9.

Table 13-9 Doby's 2019 Translated Balance Sheet under the All-current Method

	2019 (LC)	Rate ($ /LC)	2019 ($)
Cash	100	0. 4545	45. 5
Accounts receivable	650	0. 4545	295. 4
Inventory	1200	0. 4545	545. 4
Current assets	1950		886. 3
Fixed assets	1600	0. 4545	727. 2
Accumulated depreciation	(700)	0. 4545	(318. 2)
Net fixed assets	900		409. 0
Total assets	2850		1295. 3
Accounts payable	500	0. 4545	227. 3
Current debt	200	0. 4545	90. 9
Long-term debt	950	0. 4545	431. 8
Total liabilities	1650		750. 0
Common stock	400	0. 50	200. 0
Retained earnings	800		383. 3

	2019 (LC)	Rate ($/LC)	Continued 2019 ($)
Cumulative translation adjustment			(37.9)
Total equity	1200		545.4
Total liabilities and shareholders' equity	2850		1295.4

Now let's move on to the more difficult method: the temporal method. First we'll explain how inventory, cost of goods sold, fixed assets, and depreciation are actually calculated using the temporal method.

The exchange rates we use to re-measure inventory under the temporal method depend on whether the FIFO or LIFO inventory cost method is used. We'll assume Doby and Somy use the FIFO method. The beginning inventory balance is re-measured at the historical rate of $0.50, while purchases and ending inventory are re-measured at the average rate during 2019 of $0.4762. Let's start by calculating cost of goods sold (COGS) in dollars. We know that beginning inventory is LC1000, ending inventory is LC1200, and COGS is LC3300. Therefore, purchases must be 3300 + 1200 - 1000 = LC3500 (see Table 13-10).

Table 13-10 Doby's 2019 COGS in U.S. Dollars Using the Temporal Method

	LC	Rate ($/LC)	$
Beginning inventory	1000	0.50	500.0
+purchases	3500	0.4762	1666.7
-ending inventory	(1200)	0.4762	(571.4)
2019 COGS	3300		1595.3

Re-measured inventory on the balance sheet in 2019 is $571.4, and Re-measured COGS on the income statement is equal to $1595.3.

The second step is to derive net fixed assets and depreciation. Fixed asset investment is re-measured at the average rate, and beginning gross fixed assets are re-measured at the historical rate. The tricky part here is that depreciation on the income statement is re-measured at a "blended rate".

Blended rate = $(\dfrac{\text{beginning fixed assets}}{\text{ending fixed assets}}\times\text{historical rate})+(\dfrac{\text{fixed asset investment}}{\text{ending fixed assets}}\times$

average rate）

In Somy's example, the blended rate is calculated as follows:

Blended rate（in LC per \$）$=(\dfrac{800}{1600}\times2.00)+(\dfrac{800}{1600}\times2.10)=2.05$

Blended rate（in \$ per LC）$=\dfrac{1}{2.05}=0.4878$

Fixed asset investment for 2019 is equal to the difference between ending and be-ginning fixed assets: 1600−800＝800. Fixed assets for 2019 in dollars are calculated in Table 13−11.

Table 13−11　Doby's 2019 Fixed Assets in U. S. Dollars

	LC	Rate（\$/LC）	\$
Beginning fixed assets	800	0.5000	400.0
+fixed asset investment	800	0.4762	381.0
Ending fixed assets	1600		781.0

Accumulated depreciation for 2019 in dollars is calculated in Table 13−12.

Table 13−12　Doby's 2019 Depreciation in U. S. Dollars

	LC	Rate（\$/LC）	\$
Beg. acc. depreciation①	100	0.5000	50.0
+2019 depreciation	600	0.4878	292.7
End. acc. depreciation②	700		342.7

Net fixed assets on the re−measured balance sheet for 2019 is \$781−\$342.7＝\$438.3. Re−measured depreciation on the 2019 income statement is \$292.7.

---

① Beginning accumulated depreciation.

② Ending accumulated depreciation.

Now we're ready to apply the temporal method to the Somy's example.

Example: The temporal method

Suppose instead that the majority of Doby's operational, financial, and investment decisions are made by corporate headquarters in the United States. All other information is the same.

Use the appropriate method to translate Doby's 2019 balance sheet and income statement into U. S. dollars, given the following information for 2019:

COGS = $ 1595. 3

Inventory = $ 571. 4

Fixed assets = $ 781. 0

Accumulated depreciation = $ 342. 7

Depreciationexpense = $ 292. 7

Answer: Now U. S. dollars is the functional currency and the temporal method is applied.

Let's first calculate the translation gain/loss for 2019. Remember that with the temporal method the exposure is equal to (cash+receivables)−(payables+current and long−term debt).

Ending exposure = (100+650) − (500+200+950) = −LC900

Beginning exposure = (100+500) − (400+100+1300) = −LC1200

Change in exposure = −LC900 − (−LC1200) = LC300

Flow effect = LC300×(0. 4545−0. 4762) = − $ 6. 5

Holding gain effect = −LC1200×(0. 4545−0. 50) = $ 54. 6

Translation gain for 2019 = − $ 6. 5 + $ 54. 6 = $ 48. 1

Remember that the translation gain appears on the income statement under the temporal method. Doby's re−measured income statement using the temporal method is shown in Table 13−13.

Table 13−13 Doby's 2019 Re−measured Income Statement under the Temporal Method

	2019 (LC)	Rate ($/LC)	2019 ($)
Revenue	5000	0. 4762	2381. 0

	2019（LC）	Rate（$/LC）	2019（$）
			Continued
Cost of goods sold	−3300		−1595.3
Gross margin	1700		785.7
Other expenses	−400	0.4762	−190.5
Depreciation expense	−600		−292.7
Net income before translation gain	700		302.5
Translation gain			48.1
Net income	700		350.6

Beginning retained earnings in dollars was LC100×0.50 $/LC = $50, so ending retained earnings is $50+ $350.6= $400.6.

Doby's 2019 translated balance sheet is shown in Table 13−14.

Table 13−14 Doby's 2019 Re−measured Balance Sheet under the Temporal Method

	2019（LC）	Rate（$/LC）	2019（$）
Cash	100	0.4545	45.5
Accounts receivable	650	0.4545	295.4
Inventory	1200		571.4
Current assets	1950		912.3
Fixed assets	1600		781.0
Accumulated depreciation	−700		−342.7
Net fixed assets	900		438.3
Total assets	2850		1350.6
Accounts payable	500	0.4545	227.3
Current debt	200	0.4545	90.9
Long−term debt	950	0.4545	431.8
Total liabilities	1650		750.0
Common stock	400	0.50	200.0

	2019（LC）	Rate（$/LC）	Continued 2019（$）
Retained earnings	800		400. 6
Total equity	1200		600. 6
Total liabilities and shareholders' equity	2850		1350. 6

You should notice that the two different methods report very different results, particularly related to the size and sign of the translation gain/loss, net income (COGS and depreciation), and total assets (inventory and net fixed assets).

The two methods report such different results is because of the differing treatment of specific exchange rate asset and liability gain/losses, as shown in Table 13-15 and Table 13-16.

Table 13-15　Treatment of Exchange Rate Gains and Losses under the All-current Method

	Realized gains/losses	Unrealized gains/losses
Monetary assets and liabilities	CTA on the balance sheet	CTA on the balance sheet
Non-monetary assets (inventory and fixed assets)	CTA on the balance sheet	CTA on the balance sheet

Table 13-16　Treatment of Exchange Rate Gains and Losses under the Temporal Method

	Realized gains/losses	Unrealized gains/losses
Monetary assets and liabilities	Translation gain/loss on the income statement	Translation gain/loss on the income statement
Non-monetary assets (inventory and fixed assets)	Included in COGS and depreciation expense on the income statement	Ignored

13. 4　Financial Ratios with Different Methods

Next you are asked to compare A and B: A is the subsidiary's financial statements and ratios before translation; B is the subsidiary's translated financial statements and ratios using the all-current method. Table 13-17 is a side-by-side comparison from the Somy/Doby example of Doby's original balance sheet and income statement of 2019 and Doby's translated statements.

Table 13-17   Doby's Translated Balance Sheet and Income Statement

	2019（LC）	2019（$） all-current method
Cash	100	45.5
Accounts receivable	650	295.4
Inventory	1200	545.4
Current assets	1950	886.3
Fixed assets	1600	727.2
Accumulated depreciation	-700	-318.2
Net fixed assets	900	409.0
Total assets	2850	1295.3
Accounts payable	500	227.3
Current debt	200	91.0
Long-term debt	950	431.8
Total liabilities	1650	750.1
Common stock	400	200.0
Retained earnings	800	383.3
Cumulative translation adjustment		-37.9
Total equity	1200	545.4
Total liabilities and shareholders' equity	2850	1295.4
Revenue	5000	2381.0
Cost of goods sold	-3300	-1571.5
Gross margin	1700	809.5
Other expenses	-400	-190.5
Depreciation expense	-600	-285.7
Net income	700	333.3

13.4.1　Pure Balance Sheet and Pure Income Statement Ratios

All pure income statement and pure balance sheet ratios are unaffected by the application of the all-current method. In other words, the local currency trends and relationships are "preserved". What we mean by "pure" is that the components of the ratio all come from the balance sheet, or the components all come from the income statement.

For example, the current ratio (current assets divided by current liabilities) is a pure balance sheet ratio because both numerator and denominator are on the balance sheet and translated at the current rate. If you multiply both numerator and denominator by the same exchange rate, the rates cancel out, and you're left with the same ratio.

Table 13-18 shows a sample of typical pure balance sheet and pure income statement ratios and the actual ratio values for the Somy/Doby example. Notice that the all-current method preserves the original LC ratio in each case.

Table 13-18　Somy/Doby's Pure Balance Sheet and Pure Income Statement Ratios

Ratio	2019 (LC)	2019 ($) all current method
Pure balance sheet ratios		
Current ratio	2.79	2.79
Quick ratio	1.07	1.07
LTD-to-total capital	0.44	0.44
Pure income statement ratios		
Gross profit margin	34.0%	34.0%
Net profit margin	14.0%	14.0%

13.4.2　Mixed Balance Sheet/ Income Statement Ratios

The all-current method results in small change in mixed ratios that combine income statement and balance sheet items because the numerator and the denominator are almost always translated at different exchange rates. Don't expect the ratio to remain the same or large changes to appear.

Table 13 – 19 shows a sample of typical mixed balance sheet/income statement ratios and the actual ratio values for the Somy/Doby example. Recall that the exchange rate went from ＄0.50＝LC1.00 in 2018 to ＄0.4545＝LC1.00 in 2019, which means the local currency（LC）was depreciating. The average rate in 2019 was ＄0.4762＝LC1.00.

Table 13-19 Somy/Doby's Mixed Balance Sheet/Income Statement Ratios（Depreciating LC）

Ratio	2019（LC）	2019（＄）all current method
Return on assets	24.6%	25.7%
Return on equity	58.3%	61.0%
Total asset turnover	1.75	1.84
Inventory turnover	2.75	2.88
Accounts receivable turnover	7.69	8.06

Notice that in each case the translated ratio is larger than the original ratio. This will always be the case when the LC is depreciating because the average rate is greater than the ending rate. Because the numerator of each of the ratios is on the income statement and is translated at the（higher）average rate, and because the denominator in each ratio is on the balance sheet and is translated at the（lower）ending rate, each translated ratio is larger than the original ratio. When the LC is appreciating, each of these ratios will decrease.

Then, you are asked to compare C and D:

C. The re-measured financial statements and ratios using the temporal method.

D. The translated financial statements and ratios using the all-current method.

Table 13-20 is aside-by-side comparison from the Somy/Doby example of Doby's 2019 re-measured financial statement（using the temporal method）and translated financial statements (using the all-current method).

Table 13-20   Doby's 2019 Re-measured Balance Sheet and Income Statement

	2019 ($) temporal method	2019 ($) all-current method
Cash	45. 5	45. 5
Accounts receivable	295. 4	295. 4
Inventory	571. 4	545. 4
Current assets	912. 3	886. 3
Fixed assets	781. 0	727. 2
Accumulated depreciation	-342. 7	-318. 2
Net fixed assets	438. 3	409. 0
Total assets	1350. 6	1295. 3
Accounts payable	227. 3	227. 3
Current debt	90. 9	91. 0
Long-term debt	431. 8	431. 8
Total liabilities	750. 0	750. 1
Common stock	200. 0	200. 0
Retained earnings	400. 6	383. 3
Cumulative translation adjustment		-37. 9
Total equity	600. 6	545. 4
Total liabilities and shareholders' equity	1350. 6	1295. 4
Revenue	2381. 0	2381. 0
Cost of goods sold	-1595. 3	-1571. 5
Gross margin	785. 7	809. 5
Other expenses	-190. 5	-190. 5
Depreciation expense	-292. 7	-285. 7
Net income before translation gain	302. 5	333. 3
Translation gain	48. 1	
Net income	350. 6	333. 3

Analyzing the effect on the financial ratios of the choice of accounting method is a little more difficult in this case, but the basic procedure is as follows:

Determine whether the local currency (LC) is appreciating or depreciating.

Determine which rate (historical rate, average rate, or current rate) is used to convert the numerator under both methods. Determine whether the numerator of the ratio will be the same, larger, or smaller under the temporal method versus the all-current method.

Determine which rate (historical rate, average rate, or current rate) is used to convert the denominator under both methods. Determine whether the denominator of the ratio will be the same, larger, or smaller under the temporal method versus the all-current method.

Determine whether the ratio will increase, decrease, stay the same, or if the effect is uncertain, based on the direction of change in the numerator and the denominator.

For example, let's analyze the total asset turnover ratio, which is equal to sales divided by total assets.

Let's assume the local currency is depreciating.

The numerator (sales) is converted at the same rate (the average rate) under both methods.

The denominator (total assets) is converted at the historical rate under the temporal method and the current rate under the all-current method. If the LC is depreciating, the historical rate will be higher than the current rate, which means assets will be higher under the temporal method.

Total asset turnover will be lower under the temporal method.

Table 13-21 outlines the effect on various balance sheet and income statement accounts of each method with an appreciating and a depreciating currency.

The sign of the translation gain/loss is case-specific using either the temporal or all-current method, because it depends on whether the exposure and the change in the exposure are positive or negative, and whether the LC is appreciating or depreciating. However, we can make some general observations if the effects are in the same direction, as shown in Table 13-22.

Table 13-21   Effect of Translation Methods on Balance Sheet and Income Statement Items

	Appreciating LC		Depreciating LC	
	Temporal	All-current	Temporal	All-current
Income statement items				
revenues	same	same	same	same
COGS	lower	higher	higher	lower
Gross profit	higher	lower	lower	higher
Depreciation	lower	higher	higher	lower
Other expenses	same	same	same	same
NI before translation gain/loss	higher	lower	lower	higher
Translation gain/loss	+/−	+/−	+/−	+/−
NI after translation gain/loss	uncertain	uncertain	uncertain	uncertain
Balance sheet items				
cash	same	same	same	same
Accounts receivable	same	same	same	same
Inventory	lower	higher	higher	lower
Fixed assets	lower	higher	higher	lower
Total assets	lower	higher	higher	lower
liabilities	same	same	same	same
equity	lower	higher	higher	lower

Table 13-22   Effect of Appreciating or Depreciating Currency on Translation Gain/Loss

	Appreciating LC	Depreciating LC
Beginning exposure > 0 Change in exposure > 0	Translation gain	Translation loss
Beginning exposure > 0 Change in exposure < 0	uncertain	uncertain
Beginning exposure < 0 Change in exposure > 0	uncertain	uncertain
Beginning exposure < 0 Change in exposure < 0	Translation loss	Translation gain

We can use Table 13-21 to determine the effect on a selected set of common ratios, as shown in Table 13-23. In some cases, the effect on the ratio is uncertain because the change in the numerator and denominator are in the same direction or the change in one component is uncertain.

Table 13-23 Effect of Translation Methods on Selected Financial Ratios

	Appreciating local currency		Depreciating local currency	
	Temporal	All-current	Temporal	All-current
Liquidity ratios				
Current ratio	lower	higher	higher	lower
Quick ratio	same	same	same	same
A/R turnover	same	same	same	same
Inventory turnover	uncertain	uncertain	uncertain	uncertain
Operating deficiency ratios				
Fixed asset turnover	higher	lower	lower	higher
Total asset turnover	higher	lower	lower	higher
Profitability ratio				
Gross profit margin	higher	lower	lower	higher
Net profit margin	uncertain	uncertain	uncertain	uncertain
ROE	uncertain	uncertain	uncertain	uncertain
ROA	uncertain	uncertain	uncertain	uncertain
Financial leverage ratios				
Interest coverage	higher	lower	lower	higher
LTD-to-total capital	higher	lower	lower	higher

13.4.3 Effect on Parent Company Ratios

When parent firms and their foreign subsidiaries experience different trends and ratio characteristics, changing exchange rates will distort trends and ratios calculated from the consolidated financial data. If a local currency is appreciating, the foreign subsidiary's performance will have a greater impact on the consolidated data. When the local currency is depreciating, it will have a diminished impact. Even if there are no changes in the underlying ratios, changes in exchange rates will result in changes in the consolidated ratios. When the parent company has many subsidiaries operating under separate functional currencies, trends and ratios from the consolidated data, it may become very difficult to interpret without isolating the data by functional currency or by local currency.

本章小结

一、本章要点和难点

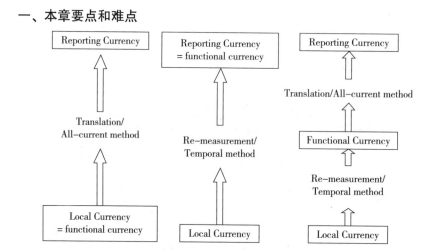

Figure 13-2 Three Methods for Re-measurement/Translation of Local Currencies

Table 13-24 Exchange Rate Usage under the Temporal and All-current Method

Account	Rate used to translate account using the two methods	
	Temporal method	All-current method
Monetary assets and liabilities	Current rate	Current rate
Non-monetary assets/liabilities	Historical rate	Current rate
Common stock and dividends	Historical rate	Historical rate

Continued

Account	Rate used to translate account using the two methods	
	Temporal method	All-current method
Equity (taken as a whole)	Blended rate	Current rate
Revenues and SG&A	Average rate	Average rate
Cost of goods sold	Historical rate	Average rate
Depreciation	Historical rate	Average rate
Net income	Blended rate	Average rate

Under the all-current method, the translation gains/losses are accumulated on the balance sheet in the equity section as part of comprehensive income in an account called the cumulative translation adjustment (CTA).

Under the temporal method, the translation gain/loss appears on the income statement.

二、Self-Test Problems

13-1 What is the translation gain or loss using the all-current method (see Table 13-25)?

Table 13-25　Data to Calculate the Traslation Cain or Loss

	Beginning of year	Average	End of year
Assets	LC6000	LC7000	LC8000
Liabilities	LC3000	LC3800	LC4600
Exchange rate (LC/ $)	4. 0	4. 5	5. 0

13-2 Subsidiary XYZ operates in the UK, and the functional currency is the British pound (£). XYZ's 2018 income statement shows £ 400 of net income and a £ 100 dividend that was paid on October 31 when the exchange rate was $ 1. 60 per £ . The current exchange rate is $ 1. 70 per £ , and the average rate is $ 1. 65 per £ . Translate the dividends at the appropriate historical rate. What will be the change in retained earnings for the period in U. S. dollars?

Chapter 14
Mergers
（并购）

Mergers represent business combinations and are associated with very complex legal, tax and synergistic issues. The initiator of the venture is referred to as the bidder or acquirer, while the opposite side of the transaction is the target. Usually, merger (兼并) generally refers to business combinations of relatively equal size, and acquisition (收购) refers to business combinations of unequal size. In this chapter, we use mergers to cover both the merger and acquisition.

Merger types:

In a horizontal merger (横向并购), the two businesses operate in the same or similar industries.

In a vertical merger (纵向并购), the acquiring company seeks to move up or down the product supply chain.

In a conglomerate merger (混合并购), the two companies operate in completely separate industries.

14.1　Merger Motivations

(1) Economies of scale.

This is exactly the strategy behind a pure horizontal merger. Imagine this scenario: two firms plan to combine even though there is no expected increasein sales. If the new entity can reduce the combined fixed costs, the average cost per unit will decrease by spreading the now lower fixed costs over the same number of units.

（2）Vertical integration.

Vertical integration seeks increased efficiencies moving forward towards the final product or backward towards the inputs. Vertical integration has the potential to increase coordination within the organization and reduce the dependency on outside suppliers.

（3）Complementary resources.

This is the classic case where the sum is greater than the individual parts. Each firm has something the other needs, and to combine is a much easier alternative than developing the "missing ingredient" on their own.

（4）Surplus cash.

Firms with large stockpiles of cash and limited growth opportunities may undertake cash-financed mergers. This is particularly true if the management is reluctant to distribute the cash to shareholders via increased dividends or stock repurchases because of tax considerations.

（5）Elimination operating inefficiencies.

Another motive for merging is simply to increase the efficiency of the target firm by replacing the current management team.

（6）Industry consolidation.

There are a lot of opportunities for realizing operating inefficiencies in industries with excess capacity and too many competitors.

（7）Net present value of a merger.

Mergers can be either financed through cash or through an exchange of shares of the combined firm. With a cash offer, the target firm will profit by the amount paid over its current share price. With a stock offer, the gains will be determined in part by the value of the combined firm because the target firm does not receive cash and just walk away, but rather retains ownership in the new firm.

In any merger that makes economic sense, the combined firmwill be worth more than the sum of the two separate firms. This difference is the "gain". The gains are then split between the bidder（B）and the target（T）. If the bidder "overpays", the target receives most of the gains. Similarly, if the bidder "underpays", the bidder receives most of the gains. The NPV, therefore, refers to the net gain to the bidder.

$$\text{Gain} = V_{BT} - (V_B + V_T) = \Delta V_{BT}$$

Where：

V_{BT} = value of combined firm

V_B = value of bidder（B）

V_T = value of target（T）

The "cost" of the merger from the bidder's perspective is how much above V_T the bidder has to offer. We will consider two cases, payment in cash and payment with stock.

1) Payment in cash.

The cost to the bidder is simply the premium above V_T:

$$\text{Cost} = \text{cash price} - V_T$$

Therefore, the NPV (from the bidder's perspective) is calculated as:

$$\text{NPV} = \text{gain} - \text{cost} = \Delta V_{BT} - (\text{cash price} - V_T)$$

Note that as long as NPV>0, the merger is value-increasing.

Example: Firm B (the bidder) has current value of $500 and seeks to acquire Firm T (the target) with a current market value of $100. The financial manager at Firm B believes that the two firms combined would be valued at $650.

Calculate the gain to the merger.

Calculate the NPV of the merger if Firm B offers $110 for Firm T.

Discuss the distribution of gains if Firm T will only accept an offer of $150.

Answer: The gain to merger = $650 - ($500 + $100) = $50.

If Firm T will accept $110, the cost of the merger is $110 - $100 = $10. Therefore, the NPV (to the bidder) is $50 - $10 = $40. If the $50 in gains to be divided, the bidder will get $40 and the target will get $10.

If Firm T will only accept the $150 offer, the cost of the merger is $150 - $100 = $50. The NPV is $50 - $50 = $0, and Firm T captures all of the gains from the merger.

2) Payment in stock.

In a stock-financed merger, the target firm receives shares of the new firm rather than cash. Accordingly, we adjust the cost of the merger formula:

$$\text{Cost} = N \times P_{BT} - V_T$$

Where:

N = number of shares the target receives

P_{BT} = price per share of combined firm after the merger announcement

Let's continue with the previous example. Suppose B has 100 shares outstanding with a price per share of $5 ($500/100 shares). Further, B exchanges 22 shares to merge with T (22× $5 = $110). We can estimate the cost of the merger as follows:

$$\text{Cost "estimate"} = 22 \times \$5 - \$100 = \$10$$

The reason we call it the cost "estimate" is that T does not receive $5 per share. It receives shares in the new firm, but we have estimated this cost by using the current market price of B. However, at the announcement of the merger, we would expect the value of BT to increase as the capital markets become aware of the economic gains that will accrue to the merged firm. Therefore, the $5 per share price understates the post-merger announcement price of BT. The market price per share after the merger is:

$$\text{Price after merger} = \frac{V_{BT}}{\text{total new shares}} = \frac{\$650}{100+22} = \$5.33$$

The cost is now computed as:

$$\text{Cost} = (22 \times \$5.33) - \$100 = \$17.26$$

As expected, the cost of the merger to the bidder has gone up, and there is now a new distribution of the $50 gain. Therefore, the NPV (from the bidder's perspective) is calculated as:

$$\text{NPV} = \text{gain} - \text{cost} = \$50 - \$17.26 = \$32.74$$

Note that this NPV is lower than $40 previously calculated from the cash offer but is still positive, which means the merger is value-increasing. Notice also that in this case the target captures $17.26 of the gains, versus $10.

There is an important lesson to learn here. If payment in cash is the method used in the merger, the distribution of the gains is unaffected by the post-merger share price of the combined firm. T's shareholders take the cash and walk away. Alternatively, the picture changes if shares are issued to T's shareholders. Now the distribution of the gains will depend on the post-merger share price.

The situation when one party has information and the other does not have is called asymmetric information. In sum, managers with private good news prefer cash mergers, and managers with private bad news prefer stock deals.

Example: Let's continue with our previous example. Suppose the managers of B privately expect the value of the combined firm to be ＄700 (＄50 higher than the public consensus of ＄650). Calculate the cost of the merger if it is stock-financed.

Answer: Since the managers privately value the firm at ＄700, the post-merger price per share is calculated as:

$$\text{Price after merger} = \frac{V_{BT}}{\text{total new shares}} = \frac{\＄700}{100+22} = \＄5.74$$

Firm B is still exchanging 22 shares for all of Firm T based on the current stock price. The cost to B is now calculated as:

$$\text{Cost} = (22 \times \＄5.74) - \＄100 = \＄26.28$$

Mergers and acquisitions of stock, and acquisitions of assets have the same goal: gain control of the target's assets. However, each approach is slightly different. In a merger, the two companies literally merge together and one company assumes all of the assets and liabilities of the other. In this case, shareholders' approval is necessary. If the payment made to the target exceeds its book value, a new entry called goodwill is created on the asset side of the balance sheet.

In an acquisition of stock, the would-be acquirer seeks control by buying stock directly from the shareholders and side-stepping the current management team. The offer can be an exchange for stock or debt securities, cash, or some combination. Once the bidder acquires a majority of stakes, control can be transferred to the bidder, and the current management team can be ousted.

An alternative approach is to purchase assets of the seller in an acquisition of assets, in which payment is made directly to the firm and not to its stockholders. The target firm retains control of its equity.

14.2 Proxy Fights (委托投票权) vs. Tender Offers (要约收购)

The most amicable mergers occur when the bidder contacts the target about its interest in merging, and friendly negotiations begin. If the target management resists the merger proposals, the acquiring firm can appeal directly to the target's shareholders to effect a change in control.

One method is to initiate a proxy fight, whereby the bidder actively seeks to "collect" and vote the shares of current shareholders via proxy. The proxy is a legal transmission of the shareholder's vote to allow another person to vote on his behalf. If the acquirer receives the support of majority shareholder, the acquirer can use its large voting block to elect its own board member at the annual meeting. Afterwards, the board would remove target management. Proxy fights are costly and difficult to win, as management has natural advantages in the voting process.

Tender offers are offers to purchase shares of the target in the open market, usually at a substantial premium above current share price. By appealing to the shareholders directly, the bidder can sidestep the existing management. If a significant number of shareholders tender their shares, the bidder may be able to pressure existing management to negotiate. On the other hand, if the bidder can acquire a majority of outstanding shares, it can nominate and elect its own board of directors and remove existing management. Management often instructs current shareholders to reject the bid for a variety of reasons: to reinforce their own job security, to initiate negotiations for a higher share price, or to start a bidding war for the company's shares among other potential acquirers.

Managers can be very creative when it comes to employing defensive measures to resist a takeover. These measures can be broadly divided into two classes: pre-offer defenses and post-offer defenses.

14.2.1 Pre-offer Defenses

(1) Staggered board.

The board of directors is split into roughly three equal-sized groups. Each group is elected for a three-year term in a staggered system: in the first year the first group is elected, the following year the next group is elected, and in the final year the third group is elected. The implications are straight-forward. In any particular year, a bidder can win at most one-third of the board seats, so it would take a potential acquirer at least two years to gain majority control of the board since the terms are overlapping for the remaining board members. This is usually longer than a bidder would want to wait and can deter a potential acquirer.

(2) Poison pill (毒丸策略).

Poison pills are extremely effective anti-takeover devices and the subject of many legal battles in their infancy. Many varieties have been used by managers over the years, but the basic premise is the same. Poison pills effectively give current shareholders the right to purchase additional shares at extremely attractive prices. This greatly increases the cost to the bidder to tender for outstanding shares.

(3) Poison put.

This anti-takeover device is different from the others, as it focuses on bondholders. These puts give bondholders the option to demand repayment of their bonds if there is a hostile takeover. This additional cash burden may fend off a would-be acquirer.

14.2.2　Post-offer Defenses

(1) Litigation.

The basic idea is to file a lawsuit against the acquirer that will require expensive and time-consuming legal efforts to fight. The typical modus operandi is to attack the merger on anti-trust grounds or some violation of securities law. The courts may disallow the merger or provide a temporary injunction delaying the merger, giving managers more time to load up their defense or seek a friendly offer.

(2) Asset restructuring.

The target firm purchases assets that effectively restructure its balance sheet. These assets may simply be ones that are unattractive to the bidder or may cause anti-trust problems if the merger now creates significant monopoly power.

(3) Liability restructuring.

The target firm restructures the equity claims on its balance sheet. The firm may issue new shares to a friendly third-party or repurchase outstanding shares. In either case, there is now a greater concentration of shares in friendly hands.

本章小结

一、本章要点与难点

（1）并购收益：$\text{Gain} = V_{BT} - (V_B + V_T) = \Delta V_{BT}$

（2）并购成本。

资金支付：$\text{Cost} = \text{cash price} - V_T$

股权支付：$\text{Cost} = N \times P_{BT} - V_T$

（3）并购利益净值：$\text{NPV} = \text{gain} - \text{cost}$

二、Self-Test Problems

14-1 Firm X has 100 shares outstanding at ＄20 per share. Firm Y also has 100 shares outstanding with a current price of ＄5 per share. Firm X offers Y's shareholders ＄8 per share in cash. Firm X's management expects the combined value of the firm to be ＄3000. How much is the expected gain and the NPV of the merger to Firm X?

14-2 Suppose Firm X in previous problem makes a stock offer for Y's outstanding shares. What is the price per share after the merger?